John Henry Newman

D1333989

Other Books by Anthony Mockler

Biography

Lions under the Throne: The Lord Chief Justices of England
Francis of Assisi: The Wandering Years
Graham Greene: Three Lives

Military History

The Mercenary Trilogy:
Mercenaries
The New Mercenaries
Hired Guns and Coups d'Etat

Our Enemies the French: The Syrian Campaign June-July 1941
Haile Selassie's War
Hostage (with Glen Dixon)

Children's

King Arthur and His Knights
Sir Yvain: The Gold-Green Knight

·

John Henry Newman

Fighter, Convert and Cardinal

Anthony Mockler

Signal

First published in 2010 by
Signal Books Limited
36 Minster Road
Oxford
OX4 1LY
www.signalbooks.co.uk

©Anthony Mockler, 2010

The right of Anthony Mockler to be identified as the author of this
work has been asserted by him in accordance with the Copyright,
Design and Patents Act, 1988.

All rights reserved. The whole of this work, including all text and
illustrations, is protected by copyright. No parts of this work may
be loaded, stored, manipulated, reproduced or transmitted in
any form or by any means, electronic or mechanical, including
photocopying and recording, or by any information, storage
and retrieval system without prior written permission from the
publisher, on behalf of the copyright owner.

A catalogue record for this book is available from the British
Library.

ISBN 978-1-904955-78-8 Paper

Production: Dorothy Martin
Cover Design: Baseline Arts
Cover Images: courtesy of Birmingham Oratory
Cartoon on p. 189 reproduced with permission of Punch Ltd/
www.punch.co.uk
Printed by the Windrush Group, Witney

Contents

This book is dedicated to Kate Fraser as a small gesture of thanks for her literally invaluable support over so many, many years.

Preface

What is the purpose of this book? To tell the story, briefly and concisely, of Newman's life and times.

Though I am a Catholic, it is not meant to be an over-respectful and over-devout tribute to Newman. On the other hand it is certainly not meant to be a debunking exercise either.

What amazed me, when I started out on this book, was how little I actually knew about Newman—and how little, in certain cases even less, my fellow-Catholics knew.

I did (though Cambridge-educated myself) know that Newman was an Oxford man through and through, a great writer and a convert. I did know (unlike an apparently well-educated Catholic friend whom I quizzed and who guessed, when pressed, that Newman had lived in the fourteenth century) that Newman was a Victorian and had written a famous *Apology*—but really I knew very little else about him. Like most English Catholics (maybe like most Catholics worldwide) I am abysmally ignorant—or was, until I began earlier this year writing this book—about the history of my own Church in my own country. (I blame for this the deplorable failure of our own priests and bishops and clergy, even the erudite ones, to instruct us—so rarely does a Sunday sermon include any hard historical facts. But that is another story.)

I was most certainly ignorant of the important fact—as I would be willing to bet most of my readers are—that Cardinal Newman only became a cardinal when he was an old, old man and apparently already near death's door—though in fact he lived another ten years. So he was Cardinal Newman only as an afterthought, not—like most Princes of the Church—appointed in his vigorous middle age.

What amazed me also, what I had absolutely no inkling of at all, is the vast number of Newman societies, Newman clubs, Newman libraries, scattered all over the globe. Newman symposiums,

Newman prayer-groups, Newman conferences, Newman essays and of course Newman schools—there seem to be an almost endless stream of these continuing now into the beginning of the century after the century after his death. It is an amazing phenomenon.

Indeed at this very moment I am writing this Preface, suitably enough (and hopefully inspired by the spirit of the great man) in an International Centre of Newman Friends. To be more specific, in what was for several years of his life Newman's own library, a converted barn out at Littlemore on the outskirts of Oxford. In the little garden outside is a head-and-shoulders of Newman carved in stone. Down the verandah is Newman's own bed-study room and oratory, meticulously preserved. Down the road is a John Henry Newman School. Newman, these days, seems to be pretty well a universal figure, frighteningly omnipresent.

And he has a worrying effect. I have it on, as they say, good authority that a recent writer on Newman, a non-Catholic, converted to Catholicism after writing the biography in question—and this despite being married to an Anglican minister. What effect will writing about Newman have on me? What effect will reading about Newman have on you? What effect indeed will publishing a book about Newman have on that traditionally impervious species, the publishers? Probably some; possibly a drastic effect; hopefully a beneficial effect. But the thought certainly makes one gulp a bit, gives one pause.

I mention the publishers because this is not a Catholic book written by a Catholic author for Catholics and published by a Catholic publishing house. The publishing house is most certainly not Catholic (even if the author happens to be) and this book is not aimed particularly at Catholics or particularly at non-Catholics but simply at all who want to know a little more about Newman and to put his life into the context of his times, and indeed of both his churches.

The book is divided into seven chapters and four intermezzos: the intermezzos being less than half the length of the chapters, and about specific, limited subjects. Furthermore, firstly, contrary to the usual practice, I have run quotations together without indicating that words or sentences are missing with the usual row of dots... This is deliberate, but not, I hope, deliberately misleading now. Secondly, I have not normally translated the Latin used here and there— Newman never did, whether in private correspondence or public writings. Thirdly, I have added as an Epilogue what could have been a Prologue to this Tale, but would, no doubt, have confused rather than amused readers if placed at the beginning. It is certainly not an essential part of the book.

Finally there is a point I would like to make as strongly as possible in this, the run-up to Newman's beatification, during which this book will make its appearance.

In certain circles an irritating and slightly sanctimonious argument is being advanced that Newman should not be made a saint (and beatification is the second, and major, step along this path) because he said that he never wanted to be and implied that he should not be.

Consider this from another angle: had Newman said that he wanted to be a saint, and implied that he ought to be—can one imagine almost any better reason for *not* making him one? Did St Francis ever dream of suggesting that he should be a saint? Of course not. If he had done so would he not, quite rightly, even with the stigmata on his hands and feet and side, have been accused of spiritual pride? And rightly so? Yet he, the most humble of men, was made a saint enormously speedily—and surely quite rightly so, whatever his own personal feelings as to his own unworthiness may have been.

Littlemore, June 2010

Chapter One

The Church that Newman was to Join

Dominic Barberi, the "simple, quaint"
Italian priest

Ambrose Phillipps was a rich, romantic, slight, undoubtedly spoilt but rather fetching young man. It came as a horrid shock to his father, a Lancashire and Leicestershire landowner, when of all things he upped and converted to Roman Catholicism—and what is more, while he was still only a schoolboy, at Edgbaston outside Birmingham. It came as even more of a shock to his uncle the Earl of Harrowby, and was yet more shocking still to his other uncle, the staunchly anti-Papist Bishop of Lichfield. For in those days, in Georgian England, Papists were few and far between—as Newman was later to put it "a *gens lucifuga*, found in corners and alleys and cellars and the housetops and in the recesses of the country".

A year later, in 1826, Ambrose tried to go up to Oxford, but Oriel College, where young Dr Newman was a Fellow and a Tutor as well as Vicar of St Mary the Virgin's the University Church, would not have a Catholic. So he went to Cambridge instead, where he was the only Catholic undergraduate in the whole university. There was one Catholic graduate in residence, Kenelm Digby (a descendant of that most loved and dignified of the Gunpowder Plotters, Sir Everard Digby, who had ended up on the scaffold a couple of hundred years earlier). Kenelm, despite his ancestry, was also a convert—though he had graduated first—and together every Sunday the two young men would ride over on horseback to St Edmund's Ware in the neighbouring county of Hertfordshire for Mass and Vespers, riding back to Cambridge in the evening, for there was no Catholic church or chapel in Cambridge at all.

Ambrose Phillipps went down without a degree. Not because he was not bright; but in order to take a degree—to graduate—all undergraduates had by law to subscribe to the 39 Articles; and to those horribly Protestant and anti-Catholic Articles of Edward VI and Elizabeth I's time Ambrose could not possibly subscribe.

His father, worried that Ambrose might become—horror of horrors—a Papist priest, encouraged him to marry. Though he did not think much of Ambrose's chosen bride Laura Clifford, of the Cliffords of Chudleigh in Devon, an Old Catholic family, for she was in his view "neither rich nor pretty", he gave them a landed estate in Leicestershire with the entrancing name of Grace Dieu. There Ambrose and Laura settled, and set out on their great scheme.

Which was nothing less than to reconvert all England to the Roman Catholic faith. And though, as readers will know, they did not succeed—and though too it would be ridiculous to suggest that it was their efforts that converted the then vicar and future Cardinal John Henry Newman—yet indirectly, as I will show, the idealistic and romantic young couple did have a hand in the final turning to Rome of that enigmatic and highly-strung, complex and affectionate, intellectual.

First, however, a brief summary of the position of Catholics in England. By the time Ambrose and Laura had married, in 1833, that position had vastly improved from what had been the case a few years before, when young Ambrose had so boldly and outrageously (because, apparently, of a sort of vision of God coming to him in the night—rather as had happened to Francis of Assisi when he had set off as a young knight towards the south of Italy to rescue princesses and been turned back by a vision calling him to other and higher things) converted to Catholicism.[1] In 1829, finally, the Catholic Emancipation Act had been passed by both Houses of Parliament and signed into law, despite much grumbling by King George IV that it was against his Coronation Oath.

What did it all mean? For centuries the Old Catholics of England had, as Newman put it, shunned the light—a tiny minority of the population of England, mainly country squires plus their retainers,

---

1 See the present author's *Francis of Assisi: The Wandering Years*. The trouble with these types of vision is that only one person knows whether they are genuine or conveniently imagined later on and used retrospectively. In Francis' case, whatever his dreams of becoming a latter-day Knight of the Round Table, they were—as he realised perfectly without the help of a vision—for him merely romantic fantasies.

lived quietly and remotely in their country houses: maintained their secret chapels, discreetly harboured priests, managed their estates, intermarried, were on good terms generally with their Protestant neighbours, but kept their distance too. They certainly—the Plowdens, the Jerninghams, the Cliffords, the Throckmortons, the Eystons, the Welds, the Scropes, the Stonors, the Bedingfields—had no thought of reconverting all England to the Faith. On the contrary, they just hoped to keep the candles dimly burning.

But gradually persecution ceased; the Penal Laws were not rigorously enforced. My own great-great-great-grandfather converted to Catholicism in the 1750s (when there were perhaps 50,000 Catholics in all England, as opposed to a nominal 5,000,000 or thereabouts now). Though as a Catholic he could not buy property, he got his brother, a C of E man, to purchase for him a small estate in Berkshire, and there, though it was still officially against the law of the land, he built a discreet little chapel on the first floor of his country house and had it consecrated to the Blessed Virgin by his friend Bishop Challoner, the Vicar Apostolic of the London District in 1773. All quite illegally—but no-one denounced him to the authorities. The tide was turning.

So in 1778 the Duke of Norfolk, nine other peers and 163 Catholic gentlemen[2] presented—much to old, cautious, conservative Bishop Challoner's horror—an Address to King George III proclaiming their loyalty to the dynasty, the constitution and indeed even to the (treacherous rather than glorious) Revolution of 1688.

Whereupon, on 3 June 1778 the First Catholic Relief Act was passed, basically abrogating the rewards for informers, the penalties of life imprisonment for Papist bishops, priests and schoolmasters found in England, and the laws forbidding Roman Catholics to purchase or inherit land—penal laws which had pretty much been a dead letter anyway—and substituting a new much less onerous Oath of Allegiance.

---

2 Not including my ancestor, who was a prosperous London tradesman and barely qualified as a gentleman, yet, despite his purchase of a country estate.

The old bishop, however, was right to be perturbed. John Wesley, founder of the Methodists, led an immediate campaign for the repeal of this (comparatively innocuous) act. Lord George Gordon, almost more of a lunatic than a fanatic, founded the Protestant Association, and the Gordon Riots of 1780 resulted: perhaps the last time in British history that London has literally been reduced to anarchy—seven days of looting, rioting, burning and mob rule, until the troops were called in and order restored. Poor Challoner died soon after, of shock and disappointment (but of old age too—he was ninety) and my ancestor, his convert and friend, hastened up to London and brought his body back for burial in the Anglican church just outside his gates where he had negotiated a family vault with the local vicar.

"Anno Domini 1781, January 22," noted the latter in his Parish Register. "Buried the Reverend Richard Challoner, a Popish Priest and Titular Bishop of London and Salisbury, a very pious and good man, of great learning and extensive abilities."[3] Not all was enmity and hostility, even in those days.

Despite the Gordon Riots, only a little over ten years later in 1791, came the Second Catholic Relief Act. This was much more positive. It now became legal for Catholic priests to celebrate Mass. It became legal for Catholics to build schools and to construct not yet churches but chapels, provided they were registered and had no steeples or bells; and (an interesting little additional rule) were not locked—for fear, presumably, of secret and sinister rites taking place behind closed doors.

Why had things eased off so much? Well, largely, indeed almost entirely, because of the French Revolution. At first the overthrow of the Bourbons—and of course the fall of the Bastille—had been heartily welcomed by public opinion in England. But by 1791 the first (Breton) bishop had taken refuge from the Revolution in England, and in September 1792 the brutal massacre of clergy in Paris had shocked the whole nation. A year later, in 1793 the students and seminarians of the English Catholic Colleges in Douai (to which

---

3 Mercilessly pressurised by a succession of centralising Cardinals, my great-uncle finally gave way and agreed to allow Bishop Challoner's body to be transferred to Westminster Cathedral. There he and Cardinal Basil Hume now have their tombs side by side in the first chapel on the right as you go in.

the Old Catholics had long sent their sons to be educated in the Faith) had been dissolved and their inhabitants briefly imprisoned, then expelled.

The result was an enormous influx of French priests to England: 5500 (including 16 bishops) by 1797. The Establishment, shocked, treated them well. Pitt, Burke and William Wilberforce were members of the Relief Committee that handed out £2 a month to refugee priests (and £10 a month to the bishops). Most eventually returned to France, but not the English exiles. Sir Edward Smythe gave the Benedictine monks of St Gregory's, Douai, a home for twenty years at Acton Burnell in Shropshire (until they went on to found Downside and the English Benedictine Congregation in Somerset in 1814). Mr Thomas Weld was even more generous. He gave the Jesuits his mansion at Stonyhurst in Lancashire and welcomed the Trappists into his main property, Lulworth in Dorset. The secular seminarians and priests from St Omer in Douai divided—some went to Old Hall, Ware, absorbed Bishop Challoner's school and built St Edmund's[4]—in the London District. Others went to Crook Hall, near Durham in the Northern District (from where in 1808 they moved to St Cuthbert's, Ushaw—the great northern seminary for the more traditionally Catholic areas of the north of England). And soon there were not only schools but chapels and indeed churches, for the limitations restricting building to chapels only seem to have been pretty much bypassed as the French and exile priests poured in.

It is impossible to exaggerate how deeply and for how very long the French Revolution affected opinion in England and, of course, events all over Europe. Under the Terror the Goddess of Reason triumphed—and not only in France. French troops occupied Rome, Pius VI, ruler of the Papal States as well as pope and Bishop of Rome, fled as an exile to Valence where he died in 1799. The Conclave in Venice elected his successor Pius VII in 1800. The next year, on 21 February 1801, John Henry Newman was born, eldest of six

---

4 To which Ambrose Phillipps and Kenelm Digby used to ride over from Cambridge on Sundays. Since 1688 the Catholics in England had been divided into four Districts: London, Northern, Central and Western with a Vicar Apostolic in charge of each. Thus Bishop Challoner had for many, many years been in charge of the London District (which extended into the Home Counties).

children, to a partner in a small London bank. By the time Newman was four and a half, Napoleon had been crowned emperor in Paris by a virtually enslaved Pius VII, and Lord Nelson was about to defeat the French and Spanish combined fleets at Trafalgar. By the time he was fourteen and a half (and still at school in Ealing) the Battle of Waterloo had been fought and won, Napoleon despatched to St Helena, Pius VII restored as Ruler of Rome—and Ambrose Phillipps was just six years old and still living with his father (his mother died young) at Garendon Park in Lancashire.

By the time of Catholic Emancipation, which had come up year after year since 1812 and continually been thrown out (once on its Third Reading by a single vote in the House of Lords), Newman was 28, and at last apparently settled in, if not exactly a career, at least a fine *cursus honorum,* and Ambrose Phillipps was a young bachelor of twenty, with good prospects as the only son—and better prospects now that official careers were to be opened to Roman Catholics.

The Catholic Emancipation Act of March 1829—forced on the Duke of Wellington in the Lords and Mr Pitt in the Commons through their gritted teeth as an indirect consequence of the Union with Ireland a generation earlier[5]— meant that all public offices (except the two Lord Chancellors of England and Ireland and the Lord Lieutenant of Ireland) were now open, without restriction, to Roman Catholics. It meant that they could become judges and KCs. It meant that they could sit on the bench and hold commissions in the armed forces of the Crown. It meant that, for the first time since 1688, Catholic peers could take their seats in the House of Lords. On 28 April the Duke of Norfolk, Lord Clifford and Lord Dormer did so, followed a month later by Lord Stourton, Lord Stafford, Lord Petre and Lord Arundell of Wardour. "Such fine tall lords," a bystander observed, "how have we managed so long without them?" But the novelist George Eliot put it otherwise in her *Felix Holt*: "Till the agitation about the Catholics in '29 rural Englishmen had hardly known more of Catholics than of the fossil mammoths."

---

5   Which meant in effect that Irish MPs could sometimes hold the balance of power in the House of Commons. In any case Ireland was in semi-revolutionary uproar once again.

In the 1830 General Election the first Catholic MP to take the oath was Henry Charles Howard, son and heir of the 12th Duke of Norfolk. Unlike his pious, quiet, elderly father, he was a great Whig and almost totally uninterested in religion.

The mantle of "leading Catholic layman" thus passed, in effect, to the 16th Earl of Shrewsbury, John Talbot, "Good Earl John". He was another Ambrose Phillipps in his way, as shy but much taller, as romantic but less excitable, born of a long line of Catholics, and far more noble of course. His ancestor had been that Talbot who had been excoriated by Joan of Arc at Orléans and who had eventually fought and died (together with his son and heir) at the very last battle of the Hundred Years War at Castillon-la-Bataille, as it has been called ever since, near Bordeaux, in what was once the Black Prince's fair province of Aquitaine.

He was also far, far, richer than Phillipps. Though he had been born plain John Talbot, the younger son of a younger son, he had lost his mother before he knew her at the age of one, and his elder brother at his first school—he had been expelled from his second school, St Edmund's Ware which he had found "beyond all endurance." He had then married an impoverished but ambitious and bright Irish cousin Maria Talbot in 1814, aged 23, and though he had lost his father too the following year, the year of Waterloo, and had lived humbly near Derby, when his uncle died in 1827 he had inherited vast wealth and properties in the Midlands—as well as the titles of Premier Earl of England and Ireland and Hereditary Lord High Steward of Ireland.

He and Maria moved at once into both Ingestre Hall near Stafford and Alton Lodge outside Stoke-upon-Trent. His uncle had redone, remodelled and renamed Alton Lodge as Alton Abbey and Earl John now rechristened it once again: Alton Towers.

There were no death duties in those days, of course, no inheritance tax, and in the 1830s agriculture became vastly prosperous, helped by the Industrial Revolution and by the discovery of coal on so many landed estates. Nonetheless it is quite frightening even to attempt to calculate how many millions in modern money Good Earl John must have spent on building—rebuilding that gothic fantasy Alton Towers, of course, and other country houses, but above all building

Catholic churches here there and everywhere, inspired, or bullied, by that desperate architectural fanatic Auguste Pugin, who had converted in 1835.

Together, the Good Earl's money and Pugin's fantastical genius in amazingly harmonious concordat, they built in Staffordshire alone St John's Hospital at Alton Towers—chapel, community hall, quadrangle—a massive project by the ruins of Alton Castle (which Pugin could not resist also renovating), St Wilfred's Church and Cotton College at Cotton, St Mary's Church at Uttoxeter, St Mary's at Brewood, and most famous and aesthetically successful of all, St Giles's Church at Cheadle, complete with presbytery, school and convent. And, with the earl's support, he took on the design and construction of what was to be the first cathedral built in England since Wren's building of St Paul's: St Chad's in Birmingham. For Ambrose and Laura Phillipps too, Pugin set about extending Grace Dieu and building a new Cistercian monastery, Mount St Bernard, in Charnwood Forest, Leicestershire, very near the site of a mediaeval foundation. It was financed, with grumblings, by Ambrose's long-suffering father, who bought him an additional 237 acres for the project. No doubt the fact that Laura had by now produced four grandchildren for him helped…

The Establishment—the Anglican world in general—viewed all this building and expansion with disquiet and distaste. But Shrewsbury—the Talbots—were Old Catholics; Ambrose Phillipps was a romantic young eccentric, and only too obviously under the spell of Sir Walter Scott's historical romances.[6] As for Pugin, his father was a Frenchman. It came as a real shock, however, and an awful blow, when in 1830 an Anglican clergyman converted to Rome.

Nor was this just any Anglican clergyman. This was the Reverend George Spencer, six years in orders, chaplain to Bishop Blomfield of Chester. And not just the Reverend George Spencer but the Reverend and the Honourable George Spencer, youngest son of the second Earl Spencer, First Lord of the Admiralty under Pitt, Home Secretary in the Ministry of All the Talents; himself educated

---

6 Such as *Marmion* (1808), admittedly a poem not a romance but based (wildly) on mediaeval convent life, *The Monastery* (1820) and its much more successful follow-up, another Waverley novel, *The Abbot.*

at Eton and Trinity College, Cambridge. His aunt was the famous, the beautiful, the notorious Georgiana Duchess of Devonshire, his brother Lord Althorp was to be Chancellor of the Exchequer and he, the Reverend George (who went on to Rome to be ordained as a Catholic priest on 26 May 1832) was—it is perhaps interesting to note—the great-great-great uncle of Diana, Princess of Wales, and therefore the great-great-great-great uncle of the future, *deo volente,* King of England—perhaps the only post-Reformation Catholic priest in the royal family tree.

There was no end of a hullaballoo. There were articles and letters in *The Times.* But the important thing, from a historical point of view, to cling on to here is the date: the first Anglican clergymen of note to "go over" to Rome in this epoch went over three years before the Oxford Movement was so much as launched; three years before Newman showed even the remotest interest in Rome (except as a debased form of the Primitive Church); eleven years, no less, before the first of the Oxford Movement clergymen went over; fifteen years indeed before Newman himself, *nel mezzo del camin di sua vita,* was finally, on 9 October 1845, converted—to the horror, but not the surprise, of all Oxford and indeed of all England bar the Papists. But that is the story to follow.

Meanwhile what of George Spencer? He had had, of course, to resign his living as soon as he "Romanized", and in normal circumstances he would have faced economic disaster and social disaster too. But his was not a normal case. His father generously continued his eighth child's allowance; and a Spencer with an earl for a father and a duchess for an aunt never risked total ostracism. Free, converted, ordained Father Spencer also set optimistically about the conversion of England.

With all these vast bursts of energy going into the Old Faith renewed, at one stage it looked as if England, despite centuries of prejudice, might indeed swing back towards Rome. The Irish poor were, even before the Famine, swarming across to Liverpool and parts north, to escape the desperate poverty and overcrowding of their own country. It is reckoned that even before the Napoleonic Wars had ended the number of Catholics in England had quintupled, to 250,000. Then there were the Italian missionaries, who had decided that England was now a happy hunting ground for souls.

"For my part," declared the first of these, Father Luigi Gentili, "I consider the English Mission the most difficult in Europe." He had had a near-disastrous experience on his first mission, coming over in 1837 with three fellow priests of the Institute of Charity, a new order.[7] He joined the megalomaniac, autocratic Bishop Baines, Vicar Apostolic of the Western District, at his vast extended school-cum-palace at Prior Park overlooking Bath. Like everyone who came into contact with Baines (such as the Benedictine monks of nearby Downside Abbey, who were the object of perpetual lawsuits by the bishop but still buried him in charity when, fortunately, he—who was strongly tipped for the post of the first Catholic archbishop—died[8]) Gentili quickly became disgusted and left, condemning "the scandals, the softness, the immorality". He was, like Rosmini, an ascetic intellectual—tall, very good-looking, with a mesmerising voice. "He won't do for England", said the Good Earl John when Gentili came back a second time and set himself up as chaplain to Ambrose Phillipps at Grace Dieu.

But he did do for England, in his own way. He was no pawn of the upper classes and their mediaeval dreams. He slept on a board and went out into the Leicestershire villages, unshaven, to preach. "People shout at you that they are free," he reported back, a mite ungratefully, to Rome, "but they are slaves to a nobility that wallows in opulence."

Unfortunately for the wallowing nobility, that was no longer as true in the 1840s as it had previously undoubtedly been. The agricultural slump drove Good Earl John to live, with his countess, mainly in Italy where living was cheaper. He still lived on a grand scale—his two daughters married, respectively, a *Principe* Borghese and a *Principe* Doria. But in 1840 tragedy struck the Shrewsburies. His elder daughter, Gwendolyn, *Principessa* Borghese, died of a fever, and weeks later her two sons both died of measles. This, along with the death of his only son and heir, demoralised the earl. He still supported Pugin and buildings and the Faith, and indeed Grace

---

7 Known as the Rosminians, after its founder Antonio Rosmini, still very much alive and active not only in Italy but, via a vast correspondence, all over Europe.
8 You can see his ornate tomb in the great Victorian gothic abbey church at Downside.

Dieu. But whereas before he had paid out £3000 here and £3000 there almost on Pugin's demand, now he was forced to economise and cut his donations to the occasional £1000. Pugin, who detested compromise and believed that money, like manna, would always descend on him, was baffled, angry and importunate.

Then, landing in England on Guy Fawkes Day 1841, came in the person of Father Dominic Barberi and one companion—the Passionists.

How did the Vatican view England at this time? The Sacred Congregation *De Propaganda Fide*—for propagating the Faith—was a Vatican department, reorganised in 1622, at the height of the terrible religious wars in Germany and northern Europe, and put under the control of thirteen cardinals, two prelates, a secretary and a consultor. It was, in other words, a very important department of state, with its own income, and its own palazzo in the Piazza di Spagna at the centre of Rome, run by its own cardinal prefect, often known as "the Red Pope".

Its job was (a) to spread Catholicism, and (b) to regulate ecclesiastical affairs in non-Catholic countries.

And of all the non-Catholic countries whose affairs needed regulating, the most important by far—much more important than the United States, Canada, all Africa, much of Germany, parts of Switzerland, the Balkans, all Asia except Russia, all Oceania except the Philippines—was the now (since 1800) United Kingdom of England, Scotland and Ireland—by far the greatest power in the whole world.

Propaganda (as it was generally called for obvious brevity's sake) therefore had the harsh, interesting but baffling task of sorting out all the senior clerical appointments in England, dealing with myriad disputes (usually over jurisdiction: was, for instance, a Benedictine group of monks to be entirely independent—as they wished—or subordinate to—as he wished—the local bishop?), receiving reports, often in rather bad Latin, from England, issuing decrees, and occasionally taking matters right up to the pope, who, like all Continentals, was both fascinated and baffled by the English, their manners, their customs, their diet, their wealth, and, of course, their immense political power, unshaken by all the recent upheavals in Europe. He was baffled, too, by the apparent immorality and frivolity of their upper classes (but was it play-acting?) and the worrying spread of liberalism. Usually there was an English cardinal resident in Rome, where all cardinals who did not have countries or archdioceses to run were by canon law obliged to reside; and usually that English cardinal was from one of the old families. At this period it was Cardinal Acton (who had succeeded to Cardinal Weld)—but though in a sense from an Old Catholic family of squires,[9] Acton was a very unusual Englishman, more at home in the magnificent Palazzo Acton alla Chiaja in Naples than in the Shropshire seat of Aldenham Hall. So, particularly in a period of rapid and confusing change, the cardinal prefect of Propaganda was not as much helped by the token English cardinal as he might have been.

And little wonder the Italians were baffled by English manners. When Newman was asked by a fellow don to dine with Father Spencer in Oxford, he refused because Spencer was, in his eyes, *in loco apostatae*—an apostate—and if Roman Catholics and Anglo-Catholics were to meet, "it should be in sackcloth, rather than at a pleasant party". Eventually he did allow Father Spencer to call on him and found him "gentlemanlike, mild and pleasing", so Newman, a great letter-writer all his long life, wrote to Spencer to apologise for not having accepted dinner in his company. But the apology was less of an apology than an awesome attack. "Your acts are contrary to your words," poor Father George was obliged to read. "You invite us to a union of hearts"—but—"You are leagued with our enemies. 'The voice is Jacob's voice but the hands are the hands of Esau.'" "Come not to us," perorated Newman, "with overtures for mutual prayer and

---

9 To be quite accurate, only Old Catholics in the sense that all old families in England had clearly once been Catholic in pre-Reformation days. Sir Richard Acton, 5th baronet, most unusually converted to Catholicism in the 1750s. And the cardinal's father, Sir John Acton, 6th baronet, a mercenary of sorts like his uncle the commodore before him, did not inherit the Shropshire estates and the title till 1791, when he was in his fifties and effectively prime minister to King Ferdinand IV of Sicily and Naples—his real home.

religious sympathy"—sounding rather like the present Archbishop of Canterbury at Easter 2010 in his crusty reaction to Pope Benedict's looming visit to England, the purpose of which, of course, was largely to centre on that very same Newman. (At least Dr Williams did not compare Benedict's hands to the hands of Esau—but may I offer the phrase to him as an extremely fetching soundbite?)

Propaganda, meanwhile, scratched its rather perplexed head and decided the best thing to do was to send another mission to England. As it turned out—and here it might be wise to invoke the inscrutable ways of Providence—this was probably the best decision Propaganda was to make vis-à-vis England that century. The missionaries to be sent were once again Italian: two Passionist priests.

Even Catholics are confused, let alone non-Catholics, with the multi-coloured complexity of the different orders within their Church. Black-robed Benedictines are monks, brown-robed Franciscans are friars, as are magpie-robed Dominicans. These three great traditional groups of men are regular clergy, not secular clergy. Secular are the ordinary parish priests; regulars are those belonging to an order regulated by a *regula*, a rule. The Benedictine Rule stressed stability, the Franciscan Holy Poverty, and the Dominicans, the intellectuals of the mediaeval church, preaching. The Jesuits, too, almost everyone knows of: St Ignatius of Loyola's soldiers of the Counter-Reformation. But Passionists, Redemptorists, Rosminians, Oratorians—the mind becomes confused. They all had in common that they were post-Reformation, therefore "modern" Orders, all were founded in Italy by Italians and all were eventually approved by the pope.

By Pope Benedict XIV in the case of both the Passionists[10] in 1741 and the Redemptorists[11] in 1749—in other words a generation or so before the French Revolution. The Redemptorists were a society of missionary priests founded by Alphonsus Maria Liguori of Amalfi to reconvert the wretched country people around Naples. The Passionists began with Paolo Danèi and his brother living a simple and frugal life as hermits on Mount Argentaro. Both orders spread

---

10 The Passionists' full title: The Congregation of Discalced Clerks of the Most Holy Cross and Passion of Our Lord Jesus Christ.
11 The Redemptorists: a rather pithier Congregation of The Most Holy Redeemer.

rapidly. By the time of Paolo's death—he was to be canonised as St Paul of the Cross—there were twelve Passionist houses in Italy, all closed down by Napoleon but reopened in 1814. Alphonsus Maria's Redemptorists (he later became a saint too and indeed was to be declared a Doctor of the Universal Church, somewhat to Newman's embarrassment, in 1871) were, as was fitting for a missionary group, more adventurous. They soon expanded into Russia, Poland and north Germany, where in 1808 a group of them were put under Fortress Arrest at Küstrin in the strictly Lutheran Kingdom of Prussia.

That was not a risk they faced in post-Napoleonic England. The Passionists arrived first in the person of Father Dominic Barberi and one companion, Father Amadeus. That was in 1841. Father Dominic had waited thirty years to go on the English mission to which ever since his ordination he had felt a weird (or at least barely explicable) calling. Inevitably he gravitated towards Staffordshire, and the first Passionist community in England set itself up, with Good Earl John's help, in Aston Hall near Stone on 17 February 1842.

The earl rather approved of Father Barberi, who was neither as coldly contemptuous towards the men as Father Gentili nor as magnetically charming towards their womenfolk. At Stone the Fathers, far from leading a retired, hermit-like life, went out boldly in their religious habits—an unheard-of thing in England at the time—to the surrounding villages, preached fine sermons in broken English, organised public religious processions in the streets—something almost as likely to encounter hostility then as in twenty-first-century England—and were jeered at, laughed at, pelted with mud and, occasionally, stones. It was not Prussia, but it was not pleasant.

Everyone seems, in the end, to have come to love the modest, simple, kindly Father Barberi. He was to live out his remaining seven years of life in England. In 1849 he was taken ill on that menacing new form of transport, the train, helped out at Pangbourne, laid on straw on the station by a concerned doctor and taken up and on to Reading where he died in the Railway Hotel. There were three fine houses of Passionists at his death. Father Spencer, who had left the secular priesthood three years earlier to join Father Barberi's

Passionists as a novice, succeeded the Italian as Superior.[12] But before that, roughly half-way through Father Dominic's ministry in England, had occurred the event for which, perhaps, God had filled him with that initial inexplicable Anglophiliac urge.

It was on 7 October 1845 that Newman wrote to his great friend and pupil, Henry Wilberforce, son of the Emancipator, from his country retreat at Littlemore:

> Father Dominic the Passionist is passing this way, on his way from Aston in Staffordshire to Belgium where a chapter of his order is to be held at this time. Father Dominic has had his thoughts turned to England from youth, in a distinct and remarkable way. I saw him over here for a few minutes on St John the Baptist's day last year when he came to see the chapel. He is a simple quaint man, an Italian. He is to come to Littlemore for the night as a guest of one of us whom he has admitted at Aston. He does not know of my intentions, but I shall ask of him admission into the One true fold of the Redeemer.

Dalgairns, a headstrong young man from the Channel Isles, was the one who had already been received at Aston. In the early afternoon of 8 October he took his hat and stick and was about to set off across the fields to walk the three miles into Oxford and meet Father Dominic's coach—safer travel than four years later in those days!—at The Angel in Oxford when Newman stopped him and said very quietly (and rather less pompously than he had put it to Henry Wilberforce), "When you see your friend will you tell him that I wish him to receive me into the Church of Christ?" Dalgairns answered a simple "Yes", passed the news to Father Dominic as he was dismounting from the coach, and the priest answered simply "God be praised". Neither man spoke a word more in the chaise

---

12 Until his own death, in 1864, in Scotland—England still unconverted. Father Dominic Barberi was beatified by Pope Paul VI in 1963, and the Cause of Father Ignatius Spencer (he had chosen the name Ignatius on joining the Passionists) was set in motion in 1982. Both men now lie buried side by side in the Church of St Anne's, Sutton, commonly (if very prematurely) known—for a holy nun is also buried there—as the "church of the three saints".

that they took back to Littlemore. It was, almost literally, stunning news—the most important conversion from Anglican to Catholic by far to take place in what was now Victorian England.

The rain had been pelting down all day. It was quite late at night when they arrived at the row of converted little cottages in Littlemore. Father Dominic sat down by the fire to dry his clothes. Newman entered, threw himself at the priest's feet—which must have been both embarrassing and disarming—and asked Father Dominic to hear his confession. Of that confession there is, of course but unfortunately, no record. What did Newman accuse himself of? Of no ordinary everyday sins we may be fairly sure; much more likely of spiritual pride and obstinacy in having for so long rejected the True Faith. At any rate the confession, rather understandably for a man of Newman's eminence and for an ordained Anglican priest submitting himself for the first time to the rites of judgement of Rome, left him prostrate. He had to be helped from the room to his bed.

Next morning Father Dominic received not only Newman into the Catholic Church but also two more of his younger followers, Frederick Bowles and Richard Stanton, both of whom, like Dalgairns and Ambrose St John,[13] were also in Anglican orders. He gave them all conditional baptism.[14] Next day he said Mass in their little oratory, their prayer room, and afterwards went with Dalgairns to the house of Mr Woodmason, a "gentleman of Littlemore". "There," Father Dominic recorded, "I heard his confession, and that of his wife and two daughters and received all four into the Church."

Seven converts in two days. Rather touchingly Father Dominic adds, "I was almost out of myself for joy." More baldly, Newman records in his diary for the following Sunday: "October 12. Went to Mass in St Clement's for the first time. St John, Dalgairns, Stanton and I."

---

13 Who had also, like Dalgairns, led the way by being received a few days earlier—at Prior Park. Of this little group of Newman's followers Ambrose St John, a sturdy, sensible young man, was to be Newman's most faithful companion through the long years and many upsets, as well as joys, which were to follow.

14 Normal, still, for Christian converts—a sort of fail-save device, just in case there had been any flaws in their original baptisms.

How Newman had changed since those early days at Oxford when he and his greatest undergraduate friend, John Bowden, had written, and published at their own expense, a two-canto epic on St Bartholomew's Massacre, of which the villain was a wicked priest named Clement:

> Mid the recesses of that pillar'd wall
> Stood Reverend Clement's dark confessional -
> Here blood-stained Murder faulter'd, tho' secure
> Of absolution from a faith impure -
> Mistaken worship! where the priestly plan
> In servile bondage rules degraded man.

Stirring stuff. Did Newman remember, one wonders, to mention his previous poetical thoughts and words in his confession—admittedly from almost thirty years earlier—to Father Dominic? They say no priest is ever shocked by what he hears in the confessional—but one wonders…

Chapter Two

Young Mr Newman

The Academic in his finery

Newman's poetry was not always so stark. Two years earlier, as a schoolboy, he had written to his sister Harriet:

> Tell Jemima [*another of his three sisters*]
> Once upon a time a
> Letter came from her pen
> And I did not answer it then:
> Therefore tell her I'm her debtor
> Of a long agreeable letter
> Of pleasant school and different places
> I'll inform her how the case is:
> Please do send me then a letter, a
> Nice epistle: Yours et cetera
>   John H Newman

A decade later, as a young don, he had refined his attractive technique and inscribed a tiny album for two young ladies:

> Fair Cousin, thy page
> is small to encage
> the thoughts which engage
> the mind of a sage
> such as I am.
>
> Still true words and plain
> of the heart not the brain
> in affectionate strain
> this book to contain
> very meet is

So I promise to be
a good Cousin to thee
and to keep safe the se-
cret I heard, although e-
v'ry one knows it

With a lyrical air
my kind thoughts I would dare
and offer what'er
beseems the news, were
I a poet.

One cannot become a saint (as Newman now is likely to become) for writing agreeable light verse. (And despite his last-line denial Newman was to become a poet, and a great poet too, though much later in life and with the fear of his own death weighing heavy upon him: the poet of *The Dream of Gerontius*.)

I suppose, though, one can almost become a saint by preaching extraordinarily good Christian sermons.

"And now," wrote the daughter of a remote Yorkshire household, the Rectory of Hauxwell, to Mark Pattison, her brother, "I have a most glorious acquisition to tell of—Philippa has sent me a copy of Newman's *Sermons on the Festivals*." "My library is swelling," she added, "only think of my having 27 of Mr N's sermons!" Hard to imagine now those impressive times when celebrities were preachers and books of sermons—and, Heavens, Mr Newman in his lifetime was to write and preach and publish hundreds of them in almost innumerable different volumes—were bestsellers. He was a tremendous preacher in the best sense, not bombastic, nor overblown, but speaking in a low and gentle voice, agreeable to the ears, and with a conviction and choice of words agreeable to hearts and minds alike. What is more, they read very well too.

But it is as a master of English prose that Newman deserves most of all to be canonised.

His *Apologia Pro Vita Sua* is, by common consent, the greatest of all his books. It is clear, concise, not nearly as long—less than 250 pages—as many of his more directly theological or doctrinal works (though indeed all his books, including certainly one of his two novels, are semi-autobiographical or at the least have streaks of autobiography in them).

The *Apologia* is the history of Newman's religious opinions from his childhood up to his conversion, told in five chapters, with seven splendidly analytical and quite fascinating appendices. Despite the title it has nothing of an apology about it. Nowadays everyone—popes, prime ministers, presidents—seem to be apologising almost continually, for what they have done (or in many cases quite extraneously for what their predecessors have done) or for what they have failed to do. A traditional *Apologia* is a very different literary beast, a written defence against a charge or criticism in writing; and a defence that very often, as in the case of Socrates' *Apologia* and, far more virulently still, in the case of William the Silent's *Apologia* against Philip of Spain, turns to a scathing counter-assault upon the Apologist's critics and accusers.

Such was Newman's *Apologia*, written late in life when he was well into his sixties and thought (wrongly as it happened) that he had not long to live: a beautiful book, easy to read (though some parts do certainly need the reader's concentration), translated and published throughout Europe at the time, accepted then as a masterpiece of English prose, still a masterpiece now—and, as they say, available in all good bookshops. I cannot recommend it too highly to readers of this short and, by comparison alas, unstylish, unwitty, unanalytical and certainly unsaintly little book—a foothill besides an Alps of literary achievements.

But, to give readers a flavour of Newman's wonderful style I will quote here a passage not from the *Apologia* but from a letter to his mother which describes his first trip ever to the West Country, in the company of his great Oriel friend Hurrell Froude. He was immediately struck by "the extreme deliciousness of the air and the fragrance of everything".

The rocks blush into every variety of colour, the trees and fields are emeralds, and the cottages are rubies. A beetle I picked up at Torquay was as green and gold as the stone it lay upon, and a squirrel which ran up a tree here just now was not the pale reddish-brown to which I am accustomed but a bright brown-red.[1] My very hands and fingers looked rosy, like Homer's Aurora,[2] and I have been gazing on them with astonishment.

The scents are extremely fine, so very delicate yet so powerful, and the colours of the flowers as if they were all shot with white. The sweet peas especially have the complexion of a beautiful face. They trail up the wall mixed with myrtle as creepers.

As to the sunset, the Dartmoor heights look purple, and the sky close upon them, a clear orange. I have heard of the brilliancy of Cintra, and still more of the East, and I suppose this region would pale beside them; yet I am content to marvel at what I see…

And so the letter goes on. What mother nowadays could hope to receive from a thirty-year-old son or daughter such a vivid, painterly yet unsentimental description of this other-England demi-paradise? It is not Newman's usual subject; in the *Apologia* I do not think there is a single at all elaborated description of nature or indeed place, though in the thirty-two volumes of his letters and diaries published so far there must surely be equal gems of descriptive prose.

Newman led a fairly unadventurous life. He certainly never got to the East. He may have got to see with his own eyes "the brilliancy of Cintra", for he did get close to Portugal, again with Hurrell Froude and this time with his father, too, the Venerable Archdeacon Froude; and in his comparatively uneventful external life this mini-grand tour, the one real adventure in the *Boys' Own* sense of Newman's life, seems to me to be central.

---

1 Alas no reddish-brown or even brown-red squirrels in Devonshire these days—only the grey invaders.
2 The famous Homeric refrain: "When dawn appeared, the rosy-fingered child of morning." Aurora is the Latin version of the dawn.

John Henry Newman was born in London on 21 February 1801, under the sign of Aquarius and within the sound of Bow Bells. He was to be the eldest of six children—three boys and three girls. Even as a boy and a young man he seems to have been a natural leader, high-spirited, with a fierce temper that he struggled, almost always successfully, to keep under control. His mother was Jemima Foudrinier, daughter of a prosperous paper merchant of Huguenot origin. She brought to the marriage a dowry of £5000 that she managed to hold on to through all the ups and downs of the family fortunes; so that at her death she left £1000 each to her five surviving children. Mary, her youngest, the family favourite and equally high-spirited, died suddenly at Brighton aged just nineteen. Newman was twenty-seven at the time. When he was over eighty he could not think of Mary without tears coming into his eyes. She was probably the person he most loved, and his emotions were always profound and strong.

As for Newman's father, John the son of John, a straightforward conventional banker, son of a "coffee-man", the first John, who had come to London from a village in East Anglia and set up as a merchant in Leadenhall Street, there is no mystery about him. But there is a touch of mystery about the family origins. Was it of Jewish descent? Certainly Newmann—Neumann—was an extremely common Jewish name all over Europe. And certainly Catholic contemporaries thought it might be the case. The *Catholic Encyclopaedia* not long after Newman's death mentioned his cast of features—even as a young man he had a remarkably hooked nose— his skill in mathematics and music, his dislike of metaphysical speculation, grasp of the concrete and nervous temperament as indicators. Whatever the truth of the matter—and possibly modern genealogical research has now resolved this minor query—it caused no prejudice, made no difference to his life, and seems to have been totally unknown to and unthought of by the man himself. It is tempting, though, to think that he had something in common with that other great Victorian, Disraeli, and that in old age while both men kept their svelte figures Newman alone retained a full and handsome head of hair.

John Henry was baptised at St Benet Fink, a church later demolished to make way for the London Stock Exchange— God for Mammon. The family lived in some style. Home was 17 Southampton Place but also Grey Court House, Ham, a fine square Georgian house set with stabling in its own grounds in almost-rustic Richmond. John Henry was sent off to school at seven, to Dr Nicholas' private academy in Ealing. He had, all in all, a very happy childhood, spared the horrid rigours of the major public schools. The family was Church of England, evangelical but by no means hyper-religious. He was brought up, as in all evangelical households, even in those pre-Victorian times, to read the Bible and "of course," he wrote later in the *Apologia*, "I had a perfect knowledge of my Catechism". (I particularly like the "of course". Even in my childhood we knew most of the Penny Catechism by heart, if not exactly perfectly. Of how many Christian children nowadays could this, or something equivalent, be said?)

This happy self-sufficient family life came to a sudden end on 8 March 1816 when the bank of Ramsbottom, Newman and Ramsbottom suddenly failed. It was no fault of Newman's father; it came about with the general collapse of the economy at the end of the Napoleonic Wars, and we nowadays know enough about bank collapses to realise how sudden, unexpected and totally baffling such events can be. The Newman family, and particularly Mr Newman senior, nearly fifty at the time, never really recovered. He found a job that autumn managing a Hampshire brewery, and the whole family moved to Alton. It was an episode[3] that John Henry never mentioned, in later life seems to have been ashamed of, and rejected any approaches of would-be biographers for fear this "disgrace" might emerge.

Meanwhile, at the age of fifteen, two things had happened, both of enormous significance. First Newman's teenage rebelliousness, intellectual and precocious rather than active, had come to a sudden end. "I was more like a devil than a wicked boy," he later wrote. It was atheism that had tempted him. Never again.

---

3   When the bank collapsed, Mr Newman and Mr Ramsbottom Junior managed to repay depositors and so avoided the disgrace of bankruptcy. But the brewery in Alton closed, and in 1821 Mr Newman did indeed, finally, go bankrupt. It had been five downhill years and he survived only another three.

He had a profound religious experience—difficult even for him, a master of words, to describe. It was not a sudden thing; it lasted for five months. God "mercifully touched my heart" was his summary, and another element that mystified many coincided. He determined to live a single life. "A deep imagination" was how he described this decision, a fascinating phrase, as indeed is the whole subject. But to treat it here would be to diverge into a very long essay. Let me just say that I am convinced, as I think *all* Newman's major and indeed minor biographers without exception have been, that he lived a life of voluntary virginity for the love of God—a life which was not unemotional, far from it. Newman had a positive genius for friendship, both with men and women; indeed, "deep friendship" might, like "deep imagination", have been one of the watchwords of his long, long life.

He had thoughts of becoming a missionary, an adventurous thing in those days, and maybe that had influenced his imagination. But he also thought of becoming a soldier—a later snippet from that descriptive letter to his mother mentions "the depth of the valleys and the steepness of the slopes... the Duke of Wellington would be in a fidget to get some commanding point to see the country from" (rather like a young subaltern of our time back from Afghanistan mentally selecting good hull-down positions for his tanks as he drives around Devonshire). But he also thought of going to the Bar; and with his analytical mind, clear-cut reasoning and almost frightening capacity for controversy, no wonder some thought that England had missed a great Lord Chancellor[4] in Newman.

The second thing was this: despite Newman's young age, despite the family's dire finances, in view of his precocious intelligence, obvious prospects of success in life, and indeed his own intellectual self-confidence and ambition, his father was determined to send him to university.

Thanks to a friend of his father, Mr Mullins, curate of St James's Piccadilly, he was found a place at Trinity College, Oxford. "Trinity, a most gentlemanlike college," said his former headmaster, Dr

---

4 Flattering, perhaps. But in another era Newman might, it is worth considering, have been like Wolsey both Lord Chancellor and Cardinal.

Nicholas, "I am much pleased to hear it." Newman matriculated—was enrolled as a commoner—on 14 December 1816, and so began the connection with that city and that university which was to dominate his life—as he indeed dominated theirs.

Oxford was most markedly different then to what Oxford is now. It was not sprawling, it was in no way industrialised, it was a mediaeval city of colleges surrounded by green fields. The government, which now funds the university and, paying the piper, calls the tune, had nothing (or almost nothing) to do with it. Colleges were far fewer, twenty in all, with half a dozen halls of residence thrown in; and, of course, for men only. Undergraduates were far less numerous, perhaps 1200 in the whole university. There were sixty at Trinity when Newman went up, and divided into commoners, gentleman commoners, scholars and noblemen (who wore a gold headband and tassel in their caps). Fellows were the most important members of the university, younger on average than they are now; forcibly celibate, for only the Heads of Houses, the (relatively few) professors and the canons of Christ Church were permitted to marry; any Fellow who did marry had to resign his fellowship. All had to subscribe to the 39 Articles; all members of the university (or at least all who wished to graduate) were therefore members of the Church of England, and all were obliged to attend chapel in their respective colleges. For the universities (but Oxford rather more so than evangelical Cambridge, set in its puritan fens) were the power-houses of the Establishment and in particular of the Established Church. The normal *cursus honorum* for the best and brightest was: undergraduate, graduate, probationer fellow, fellow, and then ordination, followed by the gift of or appointment to a living; first as a curate, then as rector, with marriage for most at this stage, followed perhaps by an archdeaconate and eventually a bishopric and a palace and a seat in the House of Lords—or possibly even an archbishopric with palace, seat, and glory too thrown in.

There was one facet of university life that is not so different at all, particularly of undergraduate life. "They sat down," wrote Newman of a party in his first term, "with the avowed determination of each making himself drunk. I really think if anyone should ask me what qualifications were necessary for Trinity College, I should say there was only one—drink, drink, drink."

Newman was by no means a teetotaller. But he was fastidious, much younger than his fellow undergraduates and quite uninterested in drink, jollity, or debauchery. Unlike many (most?) saints, unlike St Francis, he sowed no wild oats at all.[5] He made one great friend, the easy-going Bowden, told to instruct him in the ways of the college, who at nineteen was three years his elder. They became, as Newman said, "inseparables, reading, walking and boating together". And Newman worked. He studied (he claimed never less than eight hours a day) Xenophon's *Anabasis*—a mistake, he decided he should have done Herodotus instead—and Tacitus; later Herodotus indeed and Virgil, as well as Euripides, Aeschylus, Plato, Lucretius, Livy, Euclid—and mathematics in general. For recreation he walked or boated with Bowden, played the violin, took cold baths at Holywell and went to church. Sport never interested him, though of course he could ride. At the end of his first year, though he was still only seventeen, he won a college scholarship worth an amazing £60 a year for nine years—a real triumph and a considerable help to his straitened father. Out he dashed to buy a scholar's gown. "My dear scholar!" his delighted mother wrote.

But catastrophe followed two years later in his finals. The new statutes of 1800 demanded "complete proficiency" in Greek and Latin, in Rhetoric and Moral Philosophy, in Logic and Latin Composition; plus three books for detailed examination. All this for a pass degree only; for an honours degree a higher standard was required.

Newman offered, in addition to what he had already studied, Aristotle, Homer and Polybius. He was determined on a First. He wrote long, nervous, excitable letters home to all: brothers, sisters, parents. But his nerve broke. He flunked. "It is all over," he wrote to his father, "and I have not succeeded." He could hardly believe the published class list when he saw his name did not appear at all on the mathematical side and in Classics "below the line", a miserable lower

---

5 "Almost up to the twenty-fifth year of his age," wrote Thomas of Celano of Francis, disapprovingly, "he squandered and wasted his time miserably. Indeed he outdid all his contemporaries in vanities and had come to be a promoter of evil and was more abundantly zealous for all kinds of foolishness." A very different sort of saint from Newman, then.

second, at the time the lowest possible pass. "The pain it gives me to inform you and my mother of it, I cannot express."

But Newman was resilient. All his long life he was to leap up again when he was down and dusted. The scholarship had years to run yet. He could stay on, earn money coaching and—for, rather reluctantly, he was now beginning to see himself as the breadwinner of the family in place of his failing father—give up the idea of missionary adventure, give up ambitions for the Bar, which needed (what Bowden as a son of a governor of the Bank of England had) wealth to back up the lean, expensive early years; and take Holy Orders.

Not so long afterwards, despite his failure, he boldly, almost brazenly, tried for a Fellowship at Oriel. There were eleven candidates for the two available Fellowships; a five-day exam, mainly *viva voce*, over Easter 1822, all finished on the Thursday; the results announced, by the butler of the Provost of Oriel in person, on the Friday. The butler found Newman in his rooms at Trinity playing the violin. Ever after he "felt this the twelfth of April, 1822, to be the turning point of his life, and of all days most memorable". In his diary he wrote: "I have this morning been elected Fellow of Oriel. Thank God, thank God."

There is nothing special about Oriel nowadays; an attractive college, yes, but without the prestige of Balliol or the impressive spaciousness of Christ Church. But when Newman became a fellow, Oriel was the *crème de la crème*, the Athens—or at least the Platonic Academy—of Oxford. Why, how and when exactly Oriel achieved its intellectually dominant status is another story. What matters for this story, and what mattered for John Henry Newman is that to become a fellow of Oriel was to be set up for life. Indeed, he could, and did, say he never wished anything better than "to live and die a Fellow of Oriel".

At first the new fellow was painfully shy, almost silent. "When Keble [the great John Keble, the cleverest, by repute most brilliant man in the whole university] advanced to take my hand," he wrote to Bowden, "I quite shrank and could nearly have sunk into the floor, ashamed at so great an honour."

Yet Keble was only thirty, humble and self-effacing despite his brilliant Double First, his Essay prizes and his Oriel fellowship and tutorship. Son of the rector of Coln St Aldwyn in Gloucestershire, he had himself been ordained several years earlier. Keble, in appearance rather like an early Malcolm Muggeridge, was never to become a great friend. In any case he was busy with his tutoring, his curateship and with the preparation of that book of religious poems, *The Christian Year*—one poem for each Sunday, based on the Book of Common Prayer—which was to prove an enormous publishing success[6] and make him a man whose name was known all over England and indeed the Empire.

Next year, however, among the two elected fellows was a newcomer, a little older than Newman, the third of the triumvirate whose names were always to be linked as the inspirers and leaders of the Oxford Movement. This was Edward Bouverie Pusey, a man of a very different background from Keble or Newman. His father, the youngest son of Viscount Folkestone, had changed his name to Pusey when, in 1789, the Pusey estates were bequeathed to him. And there, at the vast Pusey Mansion in the village of Pusey near Faringdon in Berkshire, Pusey was born at the turn of the century—fortunately for himself a younger son. Eton and Christ Church followed. He became a friend. "His light curly head of hair was damp with the cold water which his headaches made necessary for comfort; he walked fast… stood rather bowed… His countenance was very sweet and he spoke little."

But Pusey was probably too serious, too solemn for the high-spirited Newman, who still found himself very much alone. The Provost of Oriel, finding him on a solitary walk, gave him a kindly bow and quoted Cicero: *Nunquam minus solus quam cum solus.*

For the next twenty years, Newman's life was to centre around Oriel. They were, I would venture, the most productive years of his life, neatly split into two separate decades by his voyage with the Froudes. But it was not till 1826 that Hurrell Froude first came into his life, a tall, thin, dashing young man, his father holding the wealthy living of Dartington in Devon, who was elected fellow together with

---

6   Published in 1827—and in innumerable editions afterwards. Thanks to this, the Reverend John Keble was to be elected, in 1831, Oxford's Professor of Poetry for a four-year stint.

Robert Wilberforce, another of the Emancipator's brood of sons. "Froude," wrote Newman to his mother, "is one of the acutest and clearest and deepest men in the memory of man. I hope our election will be *in honorem Dei et Sponsae suae, Ecclesiae salutem*, as Edward II has it in our statute."

Froude was not, to begin with, so enthusiastic. "Newman," he wrote to his father the Archdeacon, "is a very nice fellow indeed, but very shy." This is rather an unexpected judgment, for by 1826 Newman had been brought out of his shell by the rumbustious Dr Whately,[7] deputed for precisely the task by the college. On 13 June 1824 he had been ordained deacon by the Bishop of Oxford[8] and taken over as curate all the active work in the poor parish of St Clement's, over Magdalen Bridge; visiting the sick, comforting the dying, knocking—which must inevitably have overcome his shyness—on countless doors in his attempts to get ignorant or indifferent or actively hostile parishioners back to attendance at church. And the following year Dr Whately, appointed by Merton College principal of St Alban's Hall, a minor affiliate, had taken Newman along with him as his vice-principal. "I am Dean, Tutor, Bursar and all," he wrote cheerfully to his mother. Indeed he was Acting Principal too in Dr Whately's frequent absences. In other words, Newman was, by 1825, running a parish and running a hall of undergraduates; and (as this was the year following that in which his father died) running a family too, for his mother and sisters, and indeed his younger brothers, were now his responsibility.

So it was just as well that in 1826 he was appointed a tutor at Oriel. One of the four college tutors, at a salary of £600 a year. That enormously helped not only himself and the poor (Newman made it a principle all his life to give one-sixth of his income to the poor) but also, above all, his family responsibilities. He financed his brother Francis at Oxford; and before the decade was out had moved his mother and sisters to Iffley on the outskirts of the city, to a house

---

7 In the first pages of the *Apologia* Newman vividly describes how his friendship with Dr Whately began, flourished, then faltered.
8 Just under a year later, on 29 May 1825, he was ordained as a priest of the Church of England.

called Rose Hill and, later, to another of the same ilk, Rose Bank.[9] But he and his fellow fellows—for he was by now becoming a leader of the younger group in the common room—took tutoring duties much more seriously than was usual. They considered themselves morally responsible for the undergraduates allotted to them, and that posed problems. "The College is filled principally with men of family, in many cases," the new Junior Tutor noted, "of fortune, I fear there exists considerable profligacy among them."

This was probably not true of Henry Wilberforce, who came up that year and whom Newman tutored. But it may have been true of Tom Mozley, also a freshman, good-looking, clever but headstrong and lazy.

It clearly took some time for Hurrell Froude to become Newman's greatest friend at Oriel. More immediately the year 1826 produced a fantastically unusual addition to the Senior Common Room in the person of Blanco White, one of the few people in the story (or indeed in England in the nineteenth century) who had begun as a Roman Catholic priest and who came over to the Church of England. Mind you, Blanco White was a total eccentric. He was a Spaniard, born in Seville of Irish descent (and his brilliantly vivid *Letters from Spain* are his chief claim to fame). He was early ordained a priest, left Spain a declared atheist but, to join Oriel, became a clergyman of the Established Church of England. He was charming, excitable, highly intelligent, and enormously well-read. He went for long walks and talks with Whately alone, with Newman alone, with Whately and Newman together. He played duets with Newman, and quartets and quintets too. He was an extraordinary, a fascinating, an exotic addition to college life, which became almost cosmopolitan.

Hurrell Froude turned out to be a fascinating fellow too. "That bright and beautiful Froude," Harriet Newman was to call him, though in the end she was to marry not Froude but his pupil, Tom Mozley. "That air of sunny cheerfulness, which is best expressed by the French word *riant*," wrote a fellow don, "never forsook him." He was yet another Old Etonian, High Church, Tory and proud of it,

9 As it happens, many years later the home until her death of Mrs Graham Greene—long-separated wife to the great writer, never divorced, a devout Catholic.

a hunting, riding, skating young don, yet enormously fond of and impressed by the shy and saintly Keble.

Though when the provost of Oriel was promoted to a bishopric and his post came up for election the following year, neither Newman nor Froude voted for Keble. "If we were electing an Angel," Newman is reported to have said, "it ought to be Keble. But we are only electing a Provost." Keble, defeated, took his defeat with a gentlemanly smile but was deeply hurt. As for Froude, this is what he then wrote of Newman: "He is to my mind by far the greatest genius of the party, and I cannot help thinking that some time or other I may get to be well acquainted with him."

And so indeed it was to happen, though their interests, their characters and, at the time, their political and religious views were so very, very different.

One result of the election of the new provost, Hawkins, was that Newman was appointed in his place vicar of St Mary the Virgin's, the University Church. This was, for Newman, a tremendous step up the ladder. St Mary's fronts onto The High in Oxford, sandwiched between All Souls and Brasenose, with the Radcliffe Camera dome tucked in elegantly behind it. You can easily identify it by the bizarre but rather wonderful baroque twisting pillars on its façade—and, inside, there is what is now described as Newman's Pulpit.

It was from there that Newman delivered his famous University sermons, every Sunday afternoon during term, from the date of his induction on 14 March 1827 to the sad day on Sunday 24 September 1843 when he preached his last sermon from "his" pulpit.[10]

Oriel's official name was, and indeed is, "the House of the Blessed Mary the Virgin in Oxford, commonly called Oriel College, of the Foundation of Edward II of famous memory, sometime King of England", and St Mary the Virgin's living was and is in its gift. Famous as the former meeting place for every sort of university ceremony, from the awarding of degrees to the meetings of Congregation to

---

10 The following day, Monday the 25th, he was to preach his very last Anglican sermon at the church he had built at Littlemore—the famous sermon entitled "The Parting of Friends".

the holding of trials (including, most famously of all, the trials of the three Protestant bishops and martyrs, Latimer, Ridley and Cranmer), it was in St Mary's that Wesley preached the sermon that started the Methodist revival, and that Keble was to preach the sermon that started, officially at least, the Oxford Movement.

Newman carefully composed his sermons, writing and rewriting the texts, and would, in his low, melodious and entrancing voice, read them out to the assembled and, as his prestige grew, often packed congregation. Those who would like to know more could do worse than read the recent (2006) volume entitled *Fifteen Sermons Preached Before the University of Oxford between 1826 and 1843.*[11] These sermons were not something Newman took lightly or extemporised or delivered in ten to fifteen minutes. Each was carefully crafted. The work of preparation involved must have been daunting. Sermon XV, the last in the OUP volume, entitled *The Theory of Development in Religious Doctrine*, is estimated to have taken an hour and a half to deliver.

That same year Newman was appointed a university examiner, Keble published *The Christian Year,* and Pusey, on being appointed Regius Professor of Hebrew, moved from Oriel to Christ Church, becoming a canon of that college (where he was to live for the rest of his days)— and married.

Bowden practising at the Bar in London, "where many men were unbelievers", married too. At first shy of Newman, his new wife came to welcome this frequent guest, whom the Bowdens would refer to as "the great one".

The next year, 1828, Newman became a senior tutor, and his intimacy with Hurrell Froude, now a junior tutor (and very popular indeed with his pupils), really began. In 1829 Tom Mozley was elected a fellow, and his younger brother James came up to Oriel as

---

11   Edited with an Introduction and Notes by James Earnest and Gerard Tracy and published by Oxford University Press (before perhaps going on to the eight volumes of Newman's *Parochial and Plain Sermons*). A word of warning: the OUP volume is 436 pages long, including four appendices, and in addition has an Introduction, brilliant and readable, of a further 118 pages.

a freshman—as Newman's pupil and a very bright one,[12] a favourite with his tutor. But 1829 was also the year when with the hullaballoo over the re-election of Peel to his Oxford University seat, Oriel, began to split into two camps. It was all to do with Catholic Emancipation, and Newman threw himself into his first public fray with enormous verve, but on (for complicated reasons) the "wrong" side. "We have achieved a glorious victory," he wrote to his mother, "their insolence has been intolerable... as to talent, Whately, with perhaps Hawkins is the only man of talent among them; as to the rest, any one of us in the Oriel Common Room will fight a dozen of them apiece—and Keble is a host."

Poor Keble, who detested rows, must have much disliked being set up as, so to speak, a one-man Brigade of Guards. And it was all very well Newman ending: "I am glad to say I have seen no ill-humour anywhere. We have been merry all through it"; but Dr Whately was not a man who could agree to disagree with an upstart protégé; and Provost Hawkins clearly resented—as what provost would not?—the challenge to his authority by his senior tutor. The (indirect) upshot was that the following year Newman, Froude and indeed Robert Wilberforce were gradually edged out as tutors. Not, of course, as fellows, but it was still a monstrous blow to pocket as well as to pride, particularly as Newman's replacement was the suspiciously latitudinarian Dr Hampden, subject to be of a future kerfuffle. The provost, who disliked Froude, dubbing him the "Boy Tutor", was personally rude to Newman, accusing him of both "favouritism", and, by implication, of poverty. But Newman, always loyal to his friends—it was his unbending characteristic, and it did mean that he expected his friends to be equally loyal to him—refused to be detached from the much more relaxed (because, of course, much wealthier) pair of Froude and Wilberforce.

To the first of whom he wrote gloomily in September, "All my plans fail." In fact it was his one major setback since becoming a fellow of Oriel, and not a bad thing either. For it set him to work on a book—a

---

12 But it was not James—though it well might have been—whom Jemima, Newman's other surviving sister, was to marry but John, the eldest son, a wealthy printer and banker of Derby. So both the Newman girls married Mozley brothers; but not until 1836—one in April, one in September.

book on the early Fathers and early Councils of the Primitive Church, and in particular on his great favourite, an Alexandrian bishop he had for years been much interested in, man and Creed alike, St Athanasius: not a great book, not even a good book, but his first.

That summer in Brighton, to which Newman rode on his Arab horse Klepper (bought, possibly, through Froude's influence), artistic Maria Giberne came into their lives. Francis Newman fell head over heels in love with her but she continually refused him, despite his black hair and piercing blue eyes. At first she disliked the eldest brother, thinking him "a stiff churchman". That changed, as she watched him closely "to see what sort of man he was". She and Newman were to become lifelong friends and great correspondents. As for Francis, foiled in love, he left Oxford to take up a post as tutor in Dublin—before becoming a Darbyite, a Plymouth Brethren, and setting off, with members of his new sect, on a wild missionary expedition into Persia. This took him off the map—and almost to his death—for no less than two years.

Francis Newman was not the only one to leave Oxford for Dublin. In 1831 Dr Whately went too, but in rather a different capacity: appointed archbishop of the city, no less. Much more of a loss from Newman's point of view, Blanco White, disgusted at having to prove his rights as a naturalised Englishman at the Peel Election, quit Oxford too, accompanying the new archbishop.

Which left Newman in effect, with only Hurrell Froude and his book. All that year and the next he worked on *The Arians of the Fourth Century*. That summer of 1832 he paid the visit to Devonshire to stay with the Froudes that so entranced him. He had been straining himself with overwork on his book, and when Froude suggested out of the blue that Newman should accompany him and his father on a winter trip to the Mediterranean—"it would set you up," wrote Hurrell—he finally accepted (provided—an important point to him—that it would not cost more than £100). Off they sailed, aboard the steam-packet *Hermes*, from Falmouth in Cornwall that December.

It would not do to follow the trip in enormous detail. Newman amused himself by writing letters (over 150 survive) and by, almost everywhere, writing poetry.[13] They sailed by the coasts of Portugal and Spain, landed at Gibraltar, were off Malta on Christmas Eve, on to Zante and Patras, to Ithaca, the greatest enchantment, where he stared for hours at the "barren huge rock…Ulysses and Argus, which I had known by heart, occupied the very isle I saw"; on to English-ruled Corfu where they attended a service at an English church on the Epiphany, "the Greek Christmas Day". Back to Malta, into quarantine at the Lazaretto for a fortnight, waving goodbye to the *Hermes,* then on to Naples via Palermo aboard a very smart Italian steamer.

Sicily fascinated Newman. "It has been a day in my life to have seen Egesta." They travelled forty-three miles by carriage, then eight or nine by mule. But "oh the miserable creatures we saw in Sicily! I never knew what human suffering was before." Naples was a disappointment. But then, up the Via Appia through the desolate and dangerous Campagna to the Eternal City.

"And now," wrote Newman to Harriet, "what can I say of Rome, but that it is the first of cities and that all I ever saw are but as dust (even dear Oxford inclusive) compared with its majesty and glory? Is it possible that so serene and lofty a place is the cage of unclean creatures?" The two Anglican clergymen (without I think, the Archdeacon) did, however, resolve to pay a visit to one of those unclean creatures. The creature's name was Nicholas Wiseman, he was a Monsignor and his cage was the English College in Via Monserrato, just off the Campo di Fiori and the Palazzo Farnese, in the heart of Rome—where indeed it still discreetly stands.

The English College, the Hospice of St Thomas of Canterbury founded in the Jubilee Year of 1350 to welcome the flood of pilgrims from England, had, 200 years later, become the seminary

---

13 The verses were printed in the *British Magazine*; then collected, and, with some of Keble's and a few by other authors, published in a volume entitled *Lyra Apostolica*. I cannot help wondering if that other great Oxford man, Philip Pullman, did not, consciously or unconsciously, with irony or without, pinch Lyra as the name of the heroine of *His Dark Materials* as some sort of snook cocked at the wicked (as he would no doubt perceive him) cardinal.

from where Dr Allen and the rector Father Persons despatched those brave young Jesuits—of whom Edmund Campion, the martyr, and John Gerard, the great escaper, are the best known pair—to almost certain captivity, torture and gruesome death in Elizabethan England. Since then it had had a mixed history. The Jesuits had been suppressed and Italian priests, unsympathetic, had taken over. Numbers had fallen off. Bishop Challoner had been promised that an English rector would be reinstated. Inevitable bureaucratic delays had been followed by the French Revolution, the Napoleonic invasion—and closure.

On 8 March 1818 the *Collegio Inglese* was finally reopened. Among the first batch of six students for the priesthood came, aged sixteen, Nicholas Patrick Wiseman. Doctor of Divinity in 1824, ordained priest in 1825, author of *Horae Syriacae* and Professor of Hebrew and Syro-Chaldaean at the Sapienza in 1827. In June 1828, aged only 26, and only ten years after he had first set foot in the college, he was appointed its rector.

To call at the English College was almost an obligatory stop for distinguished English visitors to Rome. Gladstone called there that same year; Macaulay too. For Wiseman, born in Seville (like Blanco White) to an English father and an Irish-Spanish mother, educated first at Waterford then at Ushaw under Dr Lingard, a man whom, as Newman was later to note "can speak in half a dozen languages without being detected as a foreigner in any one of them", was, despite his erudition, the very opposite of what Maria Giberne would have described as a stiff churchman. He was in every sense a large personality, tall, bulky, warm, impulsive, a lackadaisical administrator, English through and through despite his country of birth, and yet totally at home in Rome, totally devoted to the popes and the cardinals and the might and pomp and majesty of the Holy See.

"Oh that Rome were not Rome!" wrote a, for once, thoroughly-in-two-minds Newman to Jemima. "I seem to see as clear as day that a union with her is *impossible*. She is the cruel Church asking of us impossibilities, excommunicating us for disobedience and now watching and exalting over our approaching overthrow."

Yet the two young Anglicans had approached the young monsignor (they were almost exactly the same age, just in their thirties) precisely in order to see if there was any chance of union with Rome. "We made our approach to the subject as delicately as we could," noted, more moderately, Hurrell. "But we found to our dismay that not one step could be gained without swallowing the Council of Trent as a whole... Newman declares that ever since I heard that I have become a staunch Protestant,[14] which is a most base calumny on his part, though I own it has altogether changed my notions of the Roman Church and"—considerably less moderately—"made me wish for the total overthrow of their system."

Nonetheless they left the English College on good terms. Wiseman (who had had Father Spencer at the seminary for his training and ordination only months earlier and knew, therefore, that Anglican priests could indeed come over) courteously hoped that they might make a second visit to Rome in the future.

"We have a work to do," Newman "with great gravity" and perhaps a certain pomposity, countered, "in England."

True. But in the end Wiseman was right, and back to Rome, in person as well as in spirit, the Reverend Newman did indeed come.

A truly strange episode followed. The Froudes, father and son, decided to head back home overland, via France; and naturally expected Newman to finish the tour in their company. Instead, an extraordinary decision for a young and insular don who had all in all led a very sheltered existence, who had never been out of England before, and who had always been cocooned by family, friends and institutions, Newman decided that he simply had to go back. Not to the Greek islands or Malta or indeed Spain, but to Sicily—to bug-infested, bandit-ridden, extravagantly un-English Sicily. He hardly knew himself why he was so determined on it. It would have been much more in character for Hurrell Froude to have set off alone into the wild. But Newman!

---

14 Protestant, to the High Church man, was in no way equivalent to Anglican. It was a term almost of abuse in Anglo-Catholic as much as in Roman Catholic parlance.

It was late in April when he landed in Messina. And, had it not been for the devoted care of his servant and muleteer Gennaro, he might well have died in Sicily. Just like Graham Greene in Liberia,[15] he came down with fever and delirium. He had had days on muleback, nights in filthy inns, fever that came and went and seemed to climax on 4 May when Gennaro thought he was dying. The crisis over, he went on again, held up sideways on his mule by Gennaro. Finally, Gennaro found him lodgings in a private house in Castro Giovanni.

They stayed there three weeks. Newman communicated with the local doctor in Latin. He was bled, by incision, then by leeches. He was dosed every two hours with sulphur and castor oil. "All through my illness I had depended on Gennaro so much I could not bear him from the room five minutes. I used always to be crying out…Gen-no-roooo." He recovered well enough to enjoy the final ride to Palermo. "I never saw such country—the spring in its greatest luxuriance… Such bright colouring—all in tune with my reviving life."

Adventures were not quite over. Three frustrating weeks of waiting for a passage in Palermo—he visited the magnificent churches but scrupulously avoided religious ceremonies—ended on 13 June with embarkation on an orange-boat for Marseilles (and from there swift coach journeys, day and night, home). But en route, on the orange steamer, becalmed for a whole week off Sardinia in the Straits of Bonifacio, he wrote for *Lyra Apostolica* a poem that was to become famous:

> Lead, kindly light, amid the encircling gloom,
>   Lead thou me on!
> The night is dark and I am far from home
>   Lead thou me on
> Keep Thou my feet; I do not ask to see
>   The distant scene—one step enough for me.

---

15 When Graham Greene, at just about the same age but a century later, determined as an adventure to walk across Liberia, he tried to give the impression in his eventual book *Journey Without Maps* that it was a solitary journey. But in fact he took a companion with him, his cousin Barbara Greene. See the present author's *Graham Greene: Three Lives*. Graham Greene, again rather like Newman, was nursed back to life too by his African "boys" Amadu, Laminah and Mark.

One can picture Newman, leaning over the steamer's railings at night, with perhaps a lighthouse twinkling on the Sardinian coast, becalmed and eager to get home for, as he had repeated again and again when he was ill, "I have a work to do in England." Indeed, facing up to what they both felt would be a looming crisis in the Church of England when both were back in Oxford, Hurrell and Newman had gaily decided on a motto for *Lyra Apostolica*. Or, to be accurate, it was Froude who was inspired. He chose the menacing words of Achilles in the *Iliad* when the man-slaying hero returns to battle: "You shall know the difference now that I am back again."

Newman entitled his poem *The Pillar of the Cloud*. But it was to gain fame not as a poem but as a hymn; and under the title of its first three words. It has been put to a variety of tunes, none approved by its author, who reacted tactfully, however, when a bishop asked permission to add a fourth verse mentioning Christ to the original, theistic but not overtly Christian, three. It was to become Queen Victoria's favourite hymn, indeed Victorian England's too, though Newman himself always considered it to be a poem, not a hymn.

The third (and, originally, final) verse seems to be inspired more by Dartmoor walks than by Sicilian mule-rides:

> So long Thy power hath blest me, sure it still
> > Will lead me on
> O'er moor and fen, o'er crag and torrent, till
> > The night is gone;
> And with the morn those angel faces smile
> > Which I have loved long since, and lost awhile.

But what baffled many readers/hymn-singers were the final two lines. What exactly was Newman referring to when he wrote of "angel faces"? What did it mean? In his old age, in 1879, the question was put to Newman. He refused to answer: "There must be a statute of limitations for writers of verse, or it would be quite a tyranny if, in an art which is the expression not of truth, but of imagination and sentiment, one were obliged to be ready for examination on the transient states of mind which come upon one when homesick, or seasick, or in any other way sensitive or excited."

This is elegant, understandable but singularly unhelpful. Did Newman mean that it was all so long ago that he had simply forgotten? Unlikely. By this time *Lead, Kindly Light* had been incorporated into, among many other collections, *Hymns, Ancient and Modern*. And he was paternal about it: he assigned the copyright to Keble College on condition that the poem must in future be printed, *pace* Bishop Bickersteth (and the American Episcopalians who mangled the original only too freely), exactly as written with no additions. In other words he still paid attention; he cared.

I feel that the clue can be found on the first page of the *Apologia* where Newman, referring back to his feelings as a child and a boy was to write: "I thought life might be a dream, or I an Angel, and all this world a deception, my fellow-angels by a playful device concealing themselves from me, and deceiving me with the semblance of a material world." And, a little later: "...I supposed he spoke of Angels who lived in the world, as it were disguised."

This fascination with angels seems to have lingered with Newman all his life,[16] as *The Dream of Gerontius* shows. Admittedly, in the *Dream*, the Choirs of Angels are (apart from Gerontius' own Angel, who hovers) mainly in, or near, the seat of Judgment in the other world: not living in this world in disguise. The whole idea of angels playfully present in the here and now has inspired other imaginations and many Hollywood films. Did this start with Newman? Was he at least imaginatively convinced of its truth but perhaps worried about its orthodoxy? Propaganda was continually being forced to mull over Newman's orthodoxy after he had converted...

Or is the idea true? Are there angels living among us? Would this fit in, one day, as an extension perhaps of Newman's most important theory: *On the Development of Christian Doctrine*? At any rate to attribute those last two lines to fond and powerful re-awakenings of his childhood beliefs flooding back into the mind and onto the pen of a thirty-year-old vicar stranded alone in the Mediterranean seems a more likely explanation than sea-sickness while becalmed. Homesickness, nostalgia, in a sense, perhaps yes—that could be true.

---

16 Unfortunately the Four Sermons on Angels that Newman preached have survived only in note form.

Chapter Three

The Church that Newman was to Leave

Pusey – "a name, a form, and a personality"

Gladstone, that colossal figure of the Victorian world, came up from Eton to Christ Church and took a Double First at Oxford in the year before Newman set off with the Froudes. He made his name with a famous speech in the newly-founded Oxford Union. The Duke of Newcastle, impressed, offered him a seat out of the blue; and the very next year, 1832, at the age of 23 there was William Ewart Gladstone in Parliament, the first Parliament to be elected after the Great Reform Bill, sitting as a Conservative MP for Newark—yes, Conservative[1]—a disciple and soon firm friend, and junior minister, of Sir Robert Peel.

I had not realised, until I read Morley's famous biography, how Gladstone all his life was much, much more interested in Church affairs than in politics. Or, as Morley more forcefully puts it,

> It was the affinity of great natures for great issues that made Mr Gladstone from his earliest manhood onwards take and hold fast the affairs of the Churches for the object of his most absorbing interest…
>
> The mighty dispute, how wide or how narrow is the common ground between the Church of England and the Church of Rome, broke into fierce flame… a drama of so many interesting characters, strange evolutions, and of a multiple and startling climax unfolding itself to Mr Gladstone's ardent and impassioned gaze.

---

[1] The "rising hope" of the "stern and unbending Tories" as Macaulay was to describe him. For the next sixty years and more Gladstone's extraordinary political career saw him in office, out of office, resigning, reappointed, now a Tory, now a Liberal, now defeated, now resurgent—and four times prime minister.

In fact, to give readers an idea of the background to this whole chapter I can, I feel, do no better than to continue to quote Gladstone's erudite biographer—in somewhat shortened and run-together form.

What is the Church of England? To ask that question was to ask a hundred others. Was the Church a purely human creation, changing with time and circumstance, like all the other creations of the heart and brain and will of man? Were the bishops mere officers, like high ministers of mundane state or the direct lineal descendants of the first apostles? What were its relations to the councils of the first four centuries, what to the councils of the fifteenth century and the sixteenth, what to the Fathers? In the answer to this group of hard questions terrible divisions that had been long muffled and huddled away burst into view.

These are questions that seem to plague the Church of England still. Morley went on to define the four parties in the Church in a manner more vivid than any prosaic analysis of Erastians, Evangelicals, Liberals and Anglo-Catholics could be:

To the Erastian lawyer the Church was an institution erected on principles of political expediency by act of parliament.

To the school of Whately and Arnold[2] it was a corporation of divine origin, devised to strengthen men in their struggle for goodness and holiness by the association and mutual help of fellow-believers.

To the evangelical it was hardly more than a collection of congregations commended in the bible for the diffusion of the knowledge and right interpretation of the Scriptures, the commemoration of gospel events, and the linking of gospel truths to a well-ordered life.

To the high Anglican as to the Roman Catholic the Church was something very different from this; not a fabric reared by

---

2 The famous Dr Arnold, later headmaster of Rugby, but at the time a fellow of Oriel. He and Newman did not, to say the least, sympathise.

man, nor in truth any mechanised fabric at all, but a mystically appointed channel of salvation. Such was the Church Catholic and Apostolic as set out from the beginning, and of this immense mystery, this saving agency, the established Church of England was the local presence and the organ.

I will leave the reader to work out for him or herself which of these four tendencies is now dominant in the present Church of England, an interesting, possibly depressing, exercise; and to imagine how the present Archbishop of Canterbury would analyse the present situation of his flock—would the analysis be any different? For which tendency does Dr Rowan Williams, himself, intellectually, stand?

But one thing is certain: Newman and Froude, heading back to England, were members of the fourth tendency. They both believed, fiercely, emotionally, intellectually that the Church of England was the English branch of the Church Catholic and Apostolic—of which the Church of Rome was, elsewhere, the unfortunately debased representative, loaded down with too many later accretions and superstitions.

"You shall know the difference now that I am back again."

Newman was back in England, refreshed, healthy, in high spirits, on 9 July 1833. Froude, back too, gleefully christened the old high-and-dry Anglo-Catholic dons and professors the Zs. But in fact it was neither of them but the for once not so mild Keble who launched the Oxford Movement with, on Sunday 14 July,[3] a sermon from the pulpit of the University Church.

Keble's sermon certainly had a fierce enough title: *On the National Apostasy.* It was Old Testament in style, it made a stir, being delivered to the Assize judges; but the occasion was odd. Earl Grey's government had brought in a bill to reduce the (Anglican) Establishment in Ireland. In a land in which only a tenth of the population were Anglican, four

---

3 "I have ever considered and kept that day as the start of the religious movement of 1833" Newman was to write in the *Apologia*. But was it in fact really the start? Probably not; there were other events, other writings. But it is, thanks to Newman's epigram, the generally accepted, and acceptable, date.

archbishops—two more than in England—and eighteen bishops seemed, in those years of reform, a top-heavy clerical bureaucracy contrary to both fairness and common sense.

But that was not how Newman and his friends saw it. For them bishops were of the Apostolic Succession—indeed, Newman was to hold (which was to cause him considerable anguish) to the principle of "Each Bishop Pope in his own diocese". To abolish any diocese, or archdiocese, was to launch an attack on the Apostolic Succession itself.

A few days later the Bishoprics Bill became law and ten Irish bishoprics were abolished. That barely mattered. The trumpet had sounded, and the Oxford Movement began to publish the *Tracts for the Times*—short pamphlets to begin with, lengthy essays as time went on—which gave the Movement its alternative title of Tractarians.

The purpose of the Tracts was to reform the Established Church by shaking it out of its torpor. In a practical way this meant circulating the Tracts by hand, by post, in bundles, individually, on horseback if necessary, to all, or most, of the rectories in England, however remote. The movement was to last for ten years, from 1833 when it was launched with Keble's sermon till 1843 when it was ended by Newman's (entirely consistent) bowing to his bishop's authority and ceasing publication of the Tracts following the uproar caused by Tract 90.

And who were the leaders of the Movement? That is a much knottier question to answer. It was, in Professor Owen Chadwick's phrase,[4] "a movement of minds", not a Marxist-Leninist-style organisation. Many were, in a sense, leaders. But who was the moving spirit?

Clearly not Keble in any case. In Chadwick's words again: "Newman charitably rendered Keble a disservice by hailing him as the true and primary author of the Oxford Movement." Two years after his notorious sermon Keble married, resigned his Fellowship and moved to Hampshire to the living of Hurley where he was to live quietly, contentedly, obscurely and childlessly, until his death in 1866. Yet for all his obscurity it is Keble who is architecturally commemorated forever in Keble College, founded four years after

---

4 See the beautifully-written, highly intelligent *The Spirit of the Oxford Movement* by Owen Chadwick, published in 1990 by Cambridge University Press.

his death by subscription among his friends and admirers. They raised over £50,000 to found a very different sort of Oxford college from the norm, "a college in which young men may be trained in simple and religious habits, and in strict fidelity to the Church of England"—aims today totally abandoned.

Whereas Pusey only has, as his lasting memorial, Pusey House (plus library and chapel) in St Giles', flanked by Blackfriars of the Dominicans on one side and the Oxfam bookshop on the other.

Pusey, even more than Newman, was to become the bugbear of the Evangelicals, and the Puseyites, in the crisis of 1851, were suspected of treachery and Romanism. Yet as Gladstone was to put it, with authoritative relief, "It was Pusey's moral weight that prevented a catastrophe greater than any the English Church has ever experienced." By which he meant that, had Pusey and the Puseyites followed Newman in going over to Rome, then indeed the Church of England might have dissolved (or, from the Catholic point of view, been at last happily reunited). But Pusey was to die (in 1882 at Ascot Priory in Berkshire) as he had lived, an Anglican divine.

Pusey's sermons were exhaustive, plodding, delivered with eyes downcast, in a monotone; and his writings were in crabbed and solemn prose. He was a weighty scholar, but scholars are no leaders, despite Newman's almost fulsome praise.

> His great learning, his scholar-like mind, his simple devotion, his deep religious seriousness, the munificence of his charities, his Professorship, his family connections, and his easy relations with the University authorities… Dr Pusey was, to use the common expression, a host in himself. He was able to give a name, a form, and a personality to what was without him a sort of mob.

Complimentary indeed; written after almost twenty years of separation; and, probably as a direct result, Newman, Keble and Pusey were reunited for what was to turn out to be a last meeting at Hursley Vicarage, in September 1865. Keble, whom Newman at first did not recognise but found "as delightful as ever", was to die the following year. As for Pusey, Newman was shocked at the weight he had put on: "His face is not changed but it is as if you looked at him through a prodigious magnifier." They corresponded, but they were never to meet again in this life.

No, there can be no doubt about it: Newman was the leading light, the moving spirit of the Oxford Movement. It was Newman who wrote, and circulated, the first three Tracts. Tract 1, *Thoughts on the Ministerial Commission Respectfully Addressed to the Clergy*, was almost designed to have eyes popping, particularly—and despite his theological respect for them—those of the bishops. "Black event as it would be for them, yet we could not wish them a more blessed termination of their course than the spoiling of their goods, and martyrdom." One can picture the shock and horror of bishops in their palaces up and down the land or clustering in the House of Lords as they digested this call by a still-anonymous Oxford author almost for the return of the pillaging and butchering Vikings—as a form of drastic purification of a degenerate Church. Tract 5, on *Alterations in the Liturgy*, attacked "the shallow and detestable liberalism of the day" and by implication the Whig grandees, "worldly men with little personal religion, of lax conversation and lax professional principles". The prime minister, the young queen-to-be's favourite, Lord Melbourne, must have recognised himself as a target. Tract 4, damning the Dissenters, was the first Keble was to write. And it was not until Tract 18, *On Fasting*, that Pusey tried his hand.

Of course, word soon leaked as to the authors, and the correspondence that ensued was immense. Outrage mingled with admiration. But if Newman was the leading light, Hurrell Froude was the driving force. The Zs wanted the Tracts stopped altogether. Newman was shaken. "My dear Froude, I do so fear I may be self-willed in this matter of the Tracts." From Devonshire Froude put steel in his friend's backbone: "As to giving up the Tracts, the notion is odious. We must throw the Zs overboard; they are a small and, as my father says, daily diminishing party. Do keep writing to Keble and stirring his rage; he is my fire but I may be his poker."

The Tracts continued. They flourished. At their height they were selling 60,000 copies a year. They spread even to Lavington in Sussex where old Mrs Sargent, widow of the late MP for Seaford, Mrs Sargent of Lavington House and Lavington Manor, had without the slightest scruple bestowed the living (and Rectory House that went with it) on her son the Reverend John Sargent, a Cambridge man, a scholar, an Evangelical—and the father of four most beautiful daughters.

The fame of the four Miss Sargents seems to have spread far and wide among the colleges of Oxford, indeed throughout the ranks of the clergy and of the Church of England as a whole. The eldest, Emily, had already (in 1829) married Sam Wilberforce, rector of Brightstone in the Isle of Wight. Henry Wilberforce, Newman's favourite pupil, was head over heels in love with Mary, the second daughter; he was due to be ordained at Easter 1833 and take up a coveted post as curate at Lavington. But as the Reverend John was ailing, and needed a curate immediately, Henry offered the post, temporarily, to an Oxford friend of his to fill in.

Thus on 3 January 1833 the Reverend Henry Manning arrived at Lavington. Manning and Gladstone were great friends. Manning (Harrow and Balliol) got his First in 1830 and became a Fellow of Merton the next year. Gladstone (Eton and Christ Church) got his Double First in 1831 and became an MP the next year. Both were extremely privileged, extremely able, extremely intelligent—and excellent orators. Manning too had wanted to go into Parliament. His father had been MP for Evesham, and a governor of the Bank of England. Unfortunately, however, his father's private bank had crashed—like Newman's father's bank but from a much greater height. So, after a brief uninspiring spell at the Colonial Office, he had decided to abandon all hopes of a political career and take Holy Orders instead.

The young curate fell under the inspiring spell fortunately not of the second but of the third of the sylph-like sisters, Catherine. It had been an immensely lucky appointment. The Reverend John died of consumption, poor fellow, on 3 May. Old Mrs Sargent offered young Mr Manning the living in his place. And on 7 November the Reverend Sam Wilberforce joined in matrimony Henry Manning and Catherine Sargent, his sister-in-law.

Henry Wilberforce, not to be outdone, upped and married his Mary the following summer, though he was nervous of letting Newman know. Newman, he was aware, disapproved of his young disciples, the future moral and intellectual leaders of the Church, marrying. Yet when George Ryder, another of Newman's pupils, son of the Bishop of Lichfield, scooped up and married the last of the beautiful quartet, Sophia, that same summer, Newman had given his admittedly slightly unenthusiastic blessing.

"It is quite absurd to suppose," he had written, "that you are not at liberty to marry and to go into the Church—indeed I think that country parsons ought, as a general rule, to be married—and I am sure the generality of men ought, whether parsons or not. The celibate is a high state of life to which the multitude of men cannot aspire. I do not say that they who adopt it are necessarily better than others, though the noblest ethos is situated in that state." It is as clear and precise a summary of Newman's view as one can hope to find anywhere in his writings on celibacy.

Thus in a short space of time the four ravishing sisters had been snapped up: by the oldest and the youngest of the Wilberforce sons (the middle brother, Robert, a fellow of Oriel and probably the most intellectual of the three, had unfortunately for himself missed out); by the ambitious, most presentable, crisp, exquisitely groomed Manning, a fine horseman and cricketer; by George Ryder, first cousin (fortunately, as it was to turn out for himself and his wife) of Ambrose Phillipps of Grace Dieu Manor with whom this book began.

What was the fate of the four Miss Sargents? Emily, the eldest, died in 1841 long before her husband "Soapy Sam" had become Bishop of Oxford (as consolation his mother-in-law went to live with him for twenty years). Henry Wilberforce's Mary lost four of her nine children. George Ryder's Sophia had three children (and, I think, lost none). As for Archdeacon Manning—soon enough his skills were recognised and he became Archdeacon of Chichester—his Catherine died of consumption after less than four years of marriage. He never remarried and in later life he never referred to his short spell of wedded bliss. It was as if it had not happened, had been erased.

Littlemore, nowadays, is swallowed up in Greater Oxford, cheek by jowl with the notorious Blackbird Leys, just across the outer ring road, itself festooned with housing estates. The only ancient sign is an old fashioned fingerpost, happily still there, indicating "Oxford - 3 miles".

In Newman's day it was a poor decaying farming community of perhaps 200 souls. But it was attached to St Mary the Virgin's, an outlying dependency, without a church of its own. It was to become, in the 1830s, rather unexpectedly and rather inexplicably, Newman's pet project—and his third home.

He had his set of rooms at Oriel—the same set for fifteen years of his life—on the first floor in Oriel Quad, near the chapel. And it was there that he now set about holding Monday evening tea-parties for all the younger fellows and undergraduates whom the Tracts, or his sermons, or both, had inspired. Then he had rooms, too, at his mother's house in Iffley, where he often used to dine *en famille* and sleep. As such, it seems odd that he also took lodgings in Littlemore with the Barnes family just by The George pub in the one street of which the hamlet then consisted.

This was probably for three reasons: first, he needed peace and quiet and time to think; and the walk (or ride) across the fields to Littlemore and back every day gave him a breathing space. Secondly, he clearly missed the parish work that he had had a taste of as curate of St Clement's. St Mary the Virgin's was not, as the University Church, a "proper" parish in the same sense; and it is a vast mistake to consider Newman simply as a student, an intellectual, a remote man. It is perfectly clear that all his life he threw himself into the humble round of parish duties and parish pleasures, and was respected, yes, but also loved and admired, especially by his poorer parishioners.

Thirdly, without a doubt, he wanted to find an occupation for his mother and for his sisters. They bustled about with a will among the poor in Littlemore. Harriet and Jemima organised a school for the village children, and on 21 July 1835 Mrs Newman, a simple soul by all accounts, a practical mother noted both for her love of the Bible and her dislike of Rome, laid the foundation stone for the church that Newman built—Littlemore Church, the Chapel of St Mary the Virgin and St Nicholas. It was a simple edifice, seating 200, without the tower and chancel added since; and it cost Newman under £700.

Swiftly built, it was due to be consecrated the following year, in September. And so it was. But this was not the joyous occasion that it should have been, for Mrs Newman had died at the age of only sixty-three. She is buried there in a vault. Newman's memorial to his mother is in Littlemore Church now.

Mrs Newman had been too "indisposed" to attend John Mozley and Jemima's wedding earlier that spring, even though it was celebrated in nearby Iffley. Newman of course officiated. And that September Harriet married John's brother Tom, now a Fellow of Oriel—too close, thought Newman, to their mother's death, but he sent her £30 for her wedding dress and told Tom to help himself to the contents of Rose Bank. For now the family home, deserted and empty, had to be sold. It left Newman, always used to warmth and affection, lonely.

Not nearly as lonely nor indeed as desolate as another death earlier that year had left him. Hurrell Froude had died in March. Henry Wilberforce saw Newman weep ("not a common thing for him"). Hurrell, once Keble's pupil, had for ten years been Newman's greatest friend and also the cheerful activist who had poked the flickering fire of the Oxford Movement into life. He had been suffering from tuberculosis. The Mediterranean winter trip had brought a respite, not a cure. Archdeacon Froude, heartbroken in Devonshire, sent Newman and Keble bundles of Hurrell's papers to edit and, if possible, to publish.

This labour of love took the pair of them two years and resulted in four volumes published as *Froude's Remains*—four volumes, and a perfect storm of criticism. Newman compiled and wrote an introduction to the first two: a collection of letters, thoughts, sayings and sermons. Keble compiled and wrote a preface to the next two volumes, which included a long study of Thomas-à-Becket.

Meanwhile Newman, perhaps determined to have another book of his own out as well as to honour Hurrell's prejudices against Rome, threw himself into a perfect frenzy of literary activity. He became editor of *The British Critic*, prepared a series of lives of the Fathers of the Early Church, edited his own *Lectures on Justification* and set about with verve, almost with glee, producing a series of middling Tracts attacking the Romanists.

These were the basis for his second book, *The Prophetical Office of the Church*. Curiously, it came out almost simultaneously, in 1837, with Gladstone's very first book *The State in Its Relation with the Church*. Gladstone's was not a success—first books very rarely are; and Newman's first book, on *The Arians*, had been very muddled too.

As for *The Prophetical Office*, here (from page 101) to give a flavour of it is a perhaps not typical but certainly striking passage. Newman was only too keen, it seems, to show that rumours—already floating in the Oxford air—that he was veering towards Rome were totally to be blown away.

We shall find too late that we are in the arms of a pitiless and unnatural relative who will but triumph in the arts that have inveigled us within her reach. For in truth she is a Church beside herself, crafty, obstinate, wilful, malicious, cruel, unnatural as madmen are.

Or rather she may be said to resemble a demoniac— possessed with principles, thoughts, and tendencies not her own; in outward form and in natural powers what God made her but ruled by an inexorable spirit. Thus she is her real self only in name, and, till God vouchsafe to restore her, we must treat her as if she were that evil one who governs her.

Even Luther in his most poisonous tirades could hardly have ranted better—which makes what was to come the following year all the more surprising. With the publication in 1838, two years after his death, of *Froude's Remains,* the whole atmosphere utterly changed.

In the House of Lords *Froude's Remains* were denounced as "doctrines recently fashionable in Oxford". To Provost Hawkins of Oriel, Headmaster Arnold, late of Oriel, wrote of the writings of a man who was once their fellow fellow: "Its prominent characteristic is extraordinary impudence."

Gladstone and Manning, hitherto supporters of the Oxford Movement,[5] were upset, baffled by an ordained minister who could describe himself as a Catholic without the popery and a Church of England man without the Protestantism.

But what seems really to have got the Establishment's goat in *Froude's Remains* was Hurrell's attitude towards the Reformation, and the Reformers. He had always loathed and detested both it and them, and out this came, in his posthumously published works, only too repeatedly and too openly. An immediate reaction set in in Oxford: a memorial was proposed in honour of the Reformation Martyrs, a subscription list was opened, Pusey to Newman's appalled horror put down his name, and the end result was the Martyrs' Memorial that now stands at the top of St Giles', honouring Ridley, Latimer and Cranmer, Cambridge men all. "It will be a good cut against Newman," it was openly said. For everyone who mattered in Oxford knew that Newman was Froude's great friend; and everyone, almost, believed that what Froude had held Newman must necessarily hold.

With hindsight it does seem as if the publication of *Froude's Remains* marked the moment when the Oxford Movement began to lose momentum. At the time it did not seem so. At the time Newman, whatever his personal woes, still seemed almost like a God in Oxford.

Here is how J. A. Froude, Hurrell's youngest brother, just up at Oriel as an undergraduate, was to describe him:

> His appearance was striking. He was above the middle height, slight and spare. His head was large, his face remarkably like that of Julius Caesar. The forehead, the shape of the ears and nose were almost the same.
>
> I often thought of the resemblance, and believed that it extended to the temperament. In both there was an original force of character, a clearness of intellectual perception, a

---

5 Newman had written to Manning two years after his marriage asking him to find a bookseller to handle, for a percentage, sale of all the Tracts. The scheme seems to have come to nothing, but it does seem to show that Newman already acknowledged Manning's drive and flair for business.

disdain for conventionalities, a temper imperious and wilful, but along with it a most attaching gentleness, sweetness, singleness of heart and purpose.

Both were formed by nature to command others. Both had the faculty of attracting to themselves the passionate devotion of their friends and followers.

I had never then seen so impressive a person. Newman's mind was world-wide. He was interested in everything that was going on in science, in politics, in literature. He could admire enthusiastically any greatness of action and character, however remote the sphere of it from his own. Gurwood's *Despatches of the Duke of Wellington* came out just then. Newman had been reading the book, and a friend asked him what he thought of it. "Think?" he said. "It makes one burn to be a soldier."[6]

Keble had looked into no lines of thought but his own. Newman read omnivorously. With us undergraduates he was never condescending, never didactic, never authoritative, ironical he could be, but not ill-natured. He was lightness itself—and he was interesting because he never talked for talking's sake, but because he had something real to say.

We who had never seen such another man, and to whom he appeared, perhaps, at special advantage in contrast with the normal college don, came to regard Newman with the affection of pupils for an idolised master. For hundreds of young men *Credo in Newmannum* was the genuine symbol of faith.

Many years later the youngest of the Froudes was to write two novels that, in effect, blamed Newman for the loss of his own Christian faith. In turn the novels cost him his Fellowship at Exeter and his prospects, which he was to redeem by his famous subsequent work in twelve volumes entitled *The History of England from the Fall of Wolsey to the Spanish Armada*, of which, oddly, Henry VIII emerges as the hero. So this Froude was by no means a blind admirer

---

6 See page 26. I think Newman could have been in other circumstances not perhaps a Caesar, but certainly a Montgomery.

of Newman, nor was he to be a convert. We can take it that his portrayal of Newman is accurate, physically, and what he felt to be true as to the character. It is probably the best assessment of Newman that we have at the height of his Oxford fame. And I think it is in no sense an obeisance to his own dead brother's memory.

In the extraordinarily intense intellectual world of mid-Victorian Britain there were two quarterly reviews of enormous prestige and influence. One entitled, unsurprisingly, the *Quarterly Review* was uprightly Tory; the other, the *Edinburgh Review*, was famously and ferociously Whig. Rector Wiseman, of the English College in Rome, over in 1836 for a year's visit and amazed by the general intellectual torpor of the English Catholics and indeed of the Irish Catholics too, determined to found a quarterly to rival the other two. With Daniel O'Connell, the Liberator (and Newman's political bugbear), young Wiseman—he was still only in his mid-thirties—founded the *Dublin Review*. This was edited by a Tipperary journalist, Michael Quin, but despite its title always published in London. Back went Wiseman to Rome for another four years. Everyone liked Wiseman there—he was affectionately known as the "Man of Providence". Large, impulsive, warm-hearted, he may have been; but he was a learned scholar and teacher too. Back in England in the summer of 1839, he preached, he gave retreats, he met Father Spencer, and he wrote an article, a famous article, for the *Dublin Review* on St Augustine and the Donatists.

Newman, of course, remembered well his and Hurrell Froude's abortive visit to the English College in Rome seven or eight years earlier. He was not particularly disposed to accept Wiseman's arguments, or indeed any Papist arguments. But...

The Long Vacation of 1839 began early. I had put away from me the controversy with Rome for more than two years. I was returning, for the Vacation, to the course of reading which I had many years before chosen as especially my own. About the middle of June I began to study and master the history of the Monophysites. I was absorbed in the doctrinal question. It was during this course of reading *that for the first time a doubt came upon me as to the tenableness of Anglicanism*. By the end of August I was seriously alarmed.

Hardly had I brought my course of reading to a close when the *Dublin Review* of that same August was put into my hands. There was an article in it on the Donatists by Dr Wiseman with an application to Anglicanism. I read it, and did not see much in it. But my friend pointed out the palmary words of St Augustine which were contained in one of the extracts made in the *Review* and which had escaped my attention: '*Securus judicat orbis terrarum*'. He repeated those words again and again and when he had gone, they kept ringing my ears.

'*Securus judicat orbis terrarum*.' What a light was hereby thrown upon every controversy in the Church! The deliberate judgement, in which the whole Church rests and acquiesces, is an infallible prescription and a final sentence against such portions of it as protest and secede.[7] The words struck me with a power which I had never felt from any words before: *securus judicat orbis terrarum*! By those great words of the ancient Father the theory of the *Via Media* was absolutely pulverised.

Such (in a condensed form and with my italics, not his) was in Newman's own words in the *Apologia* his astonishing reaction to the article in the *Dublin Review*. Wiseman was in Rome when it was published, totally ignorant of the stir his article had caused in at least one mind.

Newman mentioned his state of mind only to two old friends.

I have seen a shadow of a hand upon the wall. The heavens had opened and closed again. The thought for the moment had been, "The Church of Rome will be found right after all;" and then it had vanished. My old convictions remained as before.

---

7 The full text of the quotation from St Augustine is: *Quapropter securus judicat orbis terrarum bonos non esse qui se dividunt ab orbe terrarum in quacumque parte orbis terrarum.* The thrust is that a Church can only be regarded as belonging to the unity of the Catholic and Apostolic Succession if the general body of Christendom recognises it as such.

This, then, was not the moment of conversion—far from it. But "down had come the *Via Media* as a definite theory or scheme. My *Prophetical Office* had come to pieces. I had a great and growing dislike, after the summer of 1839, to speak against the Roman Church, herself or her formal doctrines."

Of Newman's three great points of belief, on which the whole system of his *Via Media*, the Middle Way, was founded—the principle of dogma, the sacramental system and anti-Romanism—the last had crumbled.

In that same year, 1839, Gladstone had finally married Catherine Glynne, elder sister of Sir Stephen Glynne of Hawarden in Flintshire. He was, famously, to take over the running and the management of his mild brother-in-law's estate till Hawarden became, in effect, the Gladstone not the Glynne home.

The following year, in June, his eldest son was born. He had been with Manning in Rome the previous winter, and he asked Manning to be godfather to the baby. The other godfather was James Hope-Scott[8] "whom I had known but slightly at Eton or Oxford," noted Gladstone, but who, like Manning, "had converted his acquaintance with me into a close friendship. Both these intimacies led me forward; Hope especially had influence over me, more I think than any other person at any period of my life."

And that is saying something indeed. Generally speaking Gladstone was a person who influenced other people, not one who was influenced by them. Hope-Scott was three years younger than him. He must have had a forceful character, which Newman was to dub "wonderful".

But that was years later. At the time it was Gladstone's character that interested the world; and that character Newman would never have called "wonderful". As Morley puts it, "Mr Gladstone by the time when he was thirty, had become a man of settled opinions." St

---

8   Officially still plain James Hope at this period. He changed his name to Hope-Scott when he married, in 1847, Miss Lockhart, Sir Water Scott's granddaughter. His wife was to inherit Abbotsford six years later. Hope-Scott was himself a grandson of the Earl of Hopetoun, and son of a famous general.

Augustine, to return to the saint for a moment, had once written: "We who preach and write books write while we make progress. We learn something new every day. We dictate at the same time as we explore. We speak as we are still knocking for understanding." And that was exactly true of Newman too. He, like St Augustine, wrote; he preached; but above all he learnt something new, if not every day, every season; and, as we have just seen, he was always knocking for understanding.

Not Gladstone. "What is extraordinary in the career of this far-shining and dominant character of his age," Morley continues, "is not a development of specific opinions or dogma, or discipline, or ordnance, or article or sacrament, but the fact that with a steadfast tread he marched along the high Anglican road... The years from 1831 to 1840 Mr Gladstone marked out as an era of a marvellous uprising of religious energy throughout the land. It served the Church, he says." He had disapproved of Newman's extreme anti-Papist rhetoric, but in general he, like Hope-Scott and Manning, had supported the Tractarians.

The year 1842, however, saw Gladstone much less keen on at least one manifestation of religious energy. His only surviving sister, Helen, had been visiting "Romish Chapels" and suddenly, on May 24, Gladstone learnt that she had converted to Rome. "You are living a life of utter self-deception," the stern brother wrote, "I regard you as morally beside yourself." To his father he sent a memorandum, under a variety of headings, urging him to expel Helen from his house and board. To old Mr Gladstone's credit he resisted continuous pressure from his domineering son, and finally sent Gladstone packing with a flea in his ear. His sister's religion was her own affair, and no one, therefore, had any right to condemn her, he wrote.

That was not at all how Gladstone felt; nor indeed Archdeacon Manning. And the pair of them exchanged more and more alarmed letters as, with the publication of Tract 90, crisis enveloped the Oxford Movement.

Tract 90, the last of the Tracts, appeared in February 1841. It was written by Newman. It concerned the 39 Articles to which—attentive readers will already have noted—all members of the university had to subscribe if they wished to take a degree.

It took almost forty years and four Tudor reigns (from 1538 to 1571) for the Articles to be established. First there were 13, presented by German Lutherans to Thomas Cromwell, on the lines of the Confession of Augsburg. Shocked, Henry VIII, Defender of the Faith against that very heresiarch Luther, rejected them, and substituted the notorious Six Articles.[9] Henry died, Cranmer, Latimer, Ridley and the boy King turned Calvinist. Movable tables were substituted for altars, all the old rituals abolished, all the old decorations torn down, the real Presence denied; 43 Articles of Religion by Royal Decree were imposed. Mary came to the throne; Catholicism for five years was restored. Elizabeth, succeeding her sister, compromised with 38 Articles in 1563, the 39th being added in 1571. And there they stuck.

Newman's point was that though the 39 Articles appeared utterly to condemn "Roman doctrine", and were taken as doing so, in fact they could be interpreted in a very different, much less anti-Papist way. Everything hinged on the definition of "Roman doctrine". And here one can see both the acuteness of Newman's intellect and the ability, which might indeed have made him a great lawyer, and which reoccurs again and again throughout his writings, to unpick comforting generalisations, to strip down and analyse the component parts.

Did "Roman doctrine" mean (a) the *Catholic teaching* of the early centuries? Or (b) the *formal dogmas* of Rome as contained in the later Councils, especially the Council of Trent? Or (c) the *actual popular beliefs and usages* sanctioned by Rome in the countries in communion with it? Newman argued that (a) the *Catholic teaching* was not condemned by the 39 Articles; that (c) the *popular beliefs*, which he labelled the "doctrinal errors", were condemned; that (b) the *formal dogmas* were partly condemned, partly not. Thus, for example, Prayers for the Dead (a) were not condemned. Purgatory as prison (b) was

---

9 Notorious to the Protestants who dubbed them "the whip with six lashes". But very welcome to the Catholics. They enforced belief in Transubstantiation (on pain of the stake), clerical celibacy, auricular confession, masses for the dead. Married priests had to put away their new wives…

condemned, and as fire (c) was also condemned. But the infallibility of Ecumenical Councils (b) was not condemned.

Such careful and sophisticated arguments, backed up, of course, by massive historical references, obviously did not appeal to the solid Anglican church-goer. Mr Gladstone, more the sort of man for whom it was designed, reacted in, as might have been expected, a firm but intellectual way. He wrote:

> This No. Ninety of *Tracts for the Times* is like a repetition of *Froude's Remains* and Newman has again burned his fingers. He has in writing it placed himself quite outside the Church of England in point of spirit and sympathy… As far as regards the proposition for which he intended mainly to argue, I believe not only that he is right but that is an ABC truth of the reign of Elizabeth that the authoritative documents of the Church of England were not meant to bind all men to every opinion of their authors, and particularly that they intended to deal as gently with prepossessive thought to look towards Rome as the necessity of securing a certain amount of reformation would allow.

However:

> The terms in which Newman characterises the present state of the Church of England in his introduction are calculated to give both pain and alarm; and the whole aspect of the Tract is like the assumption of a new position.

The sequel is soon told. Four Senior Tutors got together to censure Tract 90 for "removing all fences against Rome". The Heads of Houses, in the Hebdomadal Council, issued a formal condemnation. Some 3,500 copies were sold within a fortnight—partly, of course, as a result. Bishop Bagot of Oxford, a quiet man, felt that he had to step in. A compromise was reached. Tract 90 would not be withdrawn, as the bishop at first requested. But it would be the last of the Tracts. To this Newman agreed.

Why? Why did he agree? In his own words he conjures up "this sudden storm of indignation. I was quite unprepared for the outbreak and startled at its violence. I saw indeed clearly that my place in the movement was lost; public confidence was at an end; my occupation was gone... In every part of the country and every class of society, in newspapers, in periodicals, at meetings, in pulpits, at dinner-tables, in coffee-rooms, in railway carriages I was denounced as a traitor."

Did he exaggerate? Hardly. The chapter to which Morley in his *Life of Gladstone* gives the highly disapproving title of "The Tractarian Catastrophe" was over.

Intermezzo I

Interlude in Space

The simple Anglican Church he built at
Littlemore

Newman felt that as a matter of principle, as a matter of his own principles, of his view of bishops as successors of the Apostles, and of each bishop as having infallible authority in his own diocese, he had had no choice. Not everyone felt the same, though. "What a glorious clamour it has made," wrote Maria Giberne to him. "As the Blessed Froude says somewhere, 'I deprecate a calm.' I hope it is not wrong, but I cannot for the life of me help enjoying the fun of the row."

They will know the difference, he and Froude had, like Achilles, boasted, when we return to the fray. But Froude was dead and buried now, in his quiet grave, and Newman needed calm. Achilles, notoriously, had sulked in his tent before being provoked into battle. Achilles had lost his Patroclus, Newman his Hurrell. But with Newman it was the other way round. He had fought the good fight; and now he retired to his tent.

His tent, his oasis of calm, was Littlemore. And to Littlemore he in effect withdrew from the world for the next four and a half years.

Not to sulk, however. Newman could, like Achilles, be prickly. He could, like Achilles, be proud. He could, like Achilles, estimate his own value—know that he was a leader of men. But he was not a sulker. He was not an impulsive self-centred slayer of men whose strength was in his hands. Newman's strength was in his mind. He had what Achilles never had, a keen and intense power of reflection; and a keener ability still to use his intellect. As for his hands, their strength lay in writing, not fighting.

"Never act in haste" was one of Newman's maxims; and the four and a half years at Littlemore were, in one sense, slow and uneventful years. Even before Tract 90 was published, he had come down to Littlemore for Lent, practising penance, sleeping on the floor (what

Mrs Barnes thought is not recorded), fasting, reciting the breviary every day, giving catechism classes to the young children. "I have just ended the Lenten fast," he wrote to Jemima, "and Bloxam has come up and taken tea with me. Then we went to church and with much care arranged the altar cloth. It looks beautiful. As for Mrs Barnes, she dreamed of it. Indeed we are all so happy that we are afraid of being too happy." Not intellectual but genuinely idyllic.

Bloxam had been his curate at Littlemore. He was so impressed by Newman that he had offered to take on the task without pay or stipend (and had given five stained glass windows to the church—two survive). But Bloxam had blotted his copy book. One of the few Church of England clergymen who were interested in actually seeing the Romans at work and prayer, he had paid a visit to Lord Shrewsbury at Alton Towers. And there, in the Papist Chapel, he had not only attended Mass—admittedly up in the gallery—but had been seen to bow his head at the blessing. This had been reported to his bishop; and Bloxam, reprimanded, in disgrace, had resigned his curacy. But it is thanks to Bloxam, literally a lifelong friend,[1] and his notes and letters that we know much about Newman's life at Littlemore. As a curate he may have resigned but he was still in Oxford, a Fellow of Magdalen, and he, like many Oxford dons, would often make the trip across the fields to pay a call on Newman. He bore no grudge—but despite his interest Bloxam was not, in the end, to follow where Newman led.

That same May Newman did, perhaps, for once act in haste. He bought a nine-acre field from Farmer Laffer, had plans for building on it a sort of monastery—Tom Mozley his brother-in-law was to be the architect—and planted two acres of trees. But nothing came of the scheme. It was only a pipe-dream. Newman knew little about monks and monasticism; he was never attracted, as Scott or Shrewsbury had been, by a romantic, gothic, vision of the Middle Ages. That aspect of Catholicism never stirred him.

If you go to Littlemore now, it is easy enough to find Littlemore Church. About a hundred yards to the left is an angular modern

---

1 When Newman died, he flew St George's flag at half mast on his church at Upper Beeding. Five months later he followed Newman to the grave.

V-shaped Catholic church. Further on, down the next street, you may find John Henry Newman School, built, I think, on the site of the little school that Bloxam at his own expense constructed. But of a field of two acres of trees, in the cluster of housing estates all around, there is no sign.

It is difficult enough to spot the little row of single-storey stables and run-down cottages that Newman eventually did buy from Mr Costar who ran an Oxford-to-Cambridge coach service. It was the barn that first attracted Newman; and it was to the barn that in August 1842 he finally transferred his books from Oriel.[2] The stables he converted into "cells"—small, rather Spartan rooms, half a dozen of them. And there Newman installed himself, a year and a half after the Tract 90 furore, to study, to work, to lead a quiet and austere life, to look after the parishioners in Littlemore.

He still retained his rooms at Oriel and went up to Oxford once a week to preach every Sunday afternoon at the University Church. But more and more, he withdrew. He handed over the editorship of the *British Critic* to Tom Mozley (who did not make a success of it).

Rumours, of course, spread—particularly as disciples gathered around what the villagers always knew as "Mr Newman's Cottages". Some amused Newman. "I heard yesterday that the Master of University had been assured by a lady that we offered sacrifice every morning. She knew for certain we killed something. She did not know what. Little children? Or each other? Or frogs? Spiders? What?" Some annoyed him. "There is a great fat lie, a lie to the backbone, inside and out, in all sides of it, in the *Record* of yesterday evening. It has no ultimate element of truth in it, it is born of a lie, its father and mother are lies, and all its ancestry—and, to complete it, it is about me."

In fact, as Dalgairns, one of the first young men to come and live there, put it: "It really and truly as yet is nothing more than a

---

2 The barn is now a library devoted to Newman; though his books eventually followed him to Birmingham. The whole little group of buildings is now known, rather grandiosely, as the Newman College. It was in fact leased, not bought. For a hundred years after Newman it was an almshouse, administered by the Vicars. In 1950 the Diocese of Oxford put it on the market for £2000. The Birmingham Oratory bought it, restored it, and handed it over to an order of nuns to run.

place where men who have no Fellowships may come to read under Newman's instruction and with his library which is an excellent one."

Harriet and Tom Mozley came with their little daughter Grace and loved it: "4 or 5 sets of rooms—sitting and bedroom—all on the ground floor. The kitchen is in the middle—a pretty little garden before the veranda." Newman converted one of his two rooms into a little oratory, or prayer-room, making the other a bed-sitter. Men came and went, stayed for days or weeks, or months; and as the "sets" filled up, they had to be sub-divided.

Eventually a sort of monastic routine did indeed develop. The morning was spent in study or prayer, with daily visits to Littlemore Church. They fasted till midday, and in Lent till teatime. Newman took on his share of the housework and waited at table. In the evening he would play the violin, or perhaps read aloud. At midnight they rose to recite the office of the Breviary. "Newman would never let us treat him as a superior but placed himself on a level with the youngest of us. I remember that he insisted on us never calling him Mr Newman. He would have us call him simply Newman. I do not think we ever ventured on this, though we dropped the Mr and addressed him without a name."

This is the rather touching memory of William Lockhart (a relative of that Miss Lockhart whom Hope-Scott, Gladstone's best friend, was to marry). But it was Lockhart who caused the next crisis, brought about Newman's next turning point. His parents had sent him, aged 22, to Newman because they feared he might go over to Rome. Newman took him in, on condition that he, Lockhart, promised to remain in the Church of England three years. But Lockhart could not do it. Archdeacon Manning at the time was in Oxford preaching the University Sermon. Lockhart went to him to confess his sins; Manning urged him to put himself totally under Newman's guidance.

J.A. Froude came to the library to work. Mark Pattison, future Rector of Lincoln College, stayed ten days. Ambrose St John joined the group. So did Frederick Bowles and his sister Emily, who was to become Newman's favourite correspondent. Emily was abashed when the great man himself served her cold chicken for lunch.

But then, despite his promise, William Lockhart abandoned ship after only a year. "I found it impossible to keep. With great grief, I left my dear master and made my submission to the Catholic Church."

Newman's reaction seems extreme. He felt, no doubt genuinely, that he was to blame. He had let down the Lockhart family; he had let down his bishop. So he resigned. He resigned his living at the University Church, formally, before a solicitor in London, on 18 September 1843. Six days later he preached his last sermon there, and the following day his last Anglican sermon ever, his 604th, in Littlemore Church. This was the famous sermon on "The Parting of Friends". Pusey attended. The congregation, 140 strong, included no doubt some extremely baffled villagers.

Their vicar was no longer their vicar. But he still lived, as before, in the village, and he could still be seen, with his companions, on their daily walks; and still came to pray in "his" church every day. And he still remained, as always, a clergyman in Holy Orders of the Church of England.

With hindsight, this resignation could be seen, whatever its proximate cause, as a step along the road to Rome. In February Newman had already published a formal retraction "of all the hard things which I had said against the Church of Rome". And to Maria Giberne he wrote: "I do so despair of the Church of England, I am so evidently cast off by her, and on the other hand I am so drawn to the Church of Rome that I think it *safer* as a matter of honesty not to keep my living… This is a very different thing from having the *intention* of joining the Church of Rome."

Yes, but. These are Newman's italics, not mine.

The Oxford Movement had not died with the death of the Tracts and the loss of the master. In Balliol there was an immensely fat, immensely popular Fellow, Lecturer in Logic and Mathematics, once described as a "rhinoceros in the hide of a hippopotamus", by the name of W.G. Ward. He had begun by hating the Tractarians, he had ended by saying to a priest friend, "You Roman Catholics know what it is to have a Pope. Well, Newman is my Pope." Ward, unlike his "pope", had no love or reverence for the Church of England; and, as a counter-attack on Dr Palmer of Worcester, he launched in June 1844 a ferocious pamphlet that became a massive book entitled *The Ideal of a Christian Church*. A chapter heading can give an idea: "Our Church's total neglect of her duties as guardian of and witness to morality". And that was mild compared to the content.

There was an even fiercer hullaballoo. Gladstone denounced the book in the *Quarterly Review*. The Master of Balliol paced his rooms in horror quoting to himself, "We are a corrupted Church! ... We are to sue for pardon at the feet of Rome—humbly!" Even Newman wrote to Ward that "it won't do" and to Keble that it "shocks common sense".

The Hebdomadal Board, up in arms, proposed that the university should condemn Ward's book, deprive Ward of his degrees and insist on the 39 Articles being subscribed in their original sense, thus condemning Tract 90.

The whole affair became a *cause célèbre*. Convocation met in February 1845 in the Sheldonian Theatre amidst enormous excitement. Maria Giberne wrote a letter describing it all to Jemima:

> So the Heads have flayed their victim! I suppose you have heard that when Mr Ward left the Theatre he was loudly and long cheered by the undergraduates. When the Vice-Chancellor appeared immediately after him, he was assailed with snowballs.

In fact the Sheldonian was packed, Ward's book was condemned by 777 votes to 391 and he was stripped of his degrees by a much closer 569 to 511. But when it came to the vote on Tract 90, the Proctors—like the Tribunes of the People in ancient Rome the two of them had the power of veto—stepped in and, amid cheers and roars, proclaimed: *Nobis procuratoribus Non Placet*—whereupon all proceedings automatically stopped. As a don commented, "Men who had been prepared to sacrifice Ward without a struggle recoiled in horror when they found they were to sacrifice Newman too." So great was the almost magical spell that Newman, even from a distance, still threw over Oxford.

In September 1844 Newman's oldest friend, John Bowden, died. Emotionally this seems to have been the single event that—much more than the Ward fuss—finally pushed him over. It severed his last link with his early Oxford days. He was to remain closely in touch with Mrs Bowden, and her sons, for the rest of his life. But Bowden's loss was a terrible blow. Ambrose St John took the place left vacant by the deaths first of Hurrell Froude, then of Bowden. But, steady and loyal though St John was, it was never quite the same. Bowden had been Newman's chaperone, Froude his driving force. Ambrose St John was always—except in one instance—a follower.

Newman had been devoting himself to translating St Athanasius and to preparing a vastly ambitious edition of *Lives of the English Saints*. But now, in the early months of 1845 he conducted, as it were, a written Examination of Conscience.

It began as an Essay; and it was still, when finished, entitled an Essay. But in fact it became a 400-page book: *An Essay on the Development of Christian Doctrine*, and it wafted Newman, before the year was out, onto his knees before Father Barberi and into the Catholic Church.

For Newman himself it was probably the most important book he ever wrote. And it is still the most controversial. There are modern Catholic writers and theologians who claim that Newman inspired, or at least laid the foundations for, the Second Vatican Council, via the *Essay*. Others doubt it or deny it. Feelings run high about the Second Vatican Council, its merits and its failings. And arguments from the *Essay*, passages from the *Essay* are cited, now on one side, now on the other.

But here is not the place to go into the close-knit reasoning of the first part or the historical illustrations of the second. Basically the book—it is a pity it has such an uninspiring title, but Newman seems to have been hopeless in choosing titles for his books, perhaps it was a general fault of the times—the *Essay,* is an enquiry into eighteen hundred years of the Church's history, a sort of quest that will lead Newman, he hopes, to conclude that Authority resides, and has always resided, in the Roman Catholic Church and its teachings. A conclusion to which he was drawn but to which he felt there were so many objections that before he made his final move he must examine these objections and, if possible, to his own satisfaction and to those of his like-minded readers, answer and overcome them.

He based his argument on his doctrine of antecedent probability, which (if I have understood it rightly), runs something like this: We—all mankind—manage our lives, our beliefs, our actions on the basis not of certainty but of probability. Reason alone is not a sufficient guide; and arguments, however rational are not in themselves sufficient to change men's opinions. Antecedent probability rules, quite rightly, our lives.

Thus it is probable—though it can never be mathematically proved—that there is a God. It is inherently improbable that all the truths of God's Church should be contained in the Bible. Indeed, it is more than improbable; it is unarguable that the Bible, that the initial Revelation, demands interpretation; and that, as a matter of historical fact, it has been interpreted by Authority throughout the ages, especially when matters of dispute have arisen. Are these later interpretations correct? Or are they corrupt? Correct, argued Newman, provided they fulfilled seven conditions or, as he more elegantly put it, exhibited seven Notes.[3]

These Notes he then applied, each in a chapter, to such varied topics as the Church of the Fourth Century, Purgatory, or the Assimilating Power of Sacramental Grace—and many, many more. In his own words, "from the nature of the human mind, time is necessary for the full comprehension and perfection of great ideas. This may be called the *Theory of Development of Doctrine*."

Such, vastly oversimplified, is the process of thought which led Newman to conclude that the single unified lasting teaching Body which has developed and will develop doctrine, with Authority, is, and must remain, the Roman Catholic Church.

That is how Newman's intellect was working in those early months of 1845; and that is what eventually led him—but only after

---

3 The seven Notes are: Preservation of Its Type, Continuity of Its Principles, Its Power of Assimilation, Its Logical Sequence, Anticipation of Its Future, Conservative Action Upon Its Past, and Its Chronic Vigour, of which the last is perhaps the most original: the view that corrupt opinions and practices, heresies and schisms, will always and inevitably die—fall away like dead branches off a vigorous tree.

Ambrose St John and others of his younger, simpler companions had paved the way—to the greatest turning-point; to—as has already been described—his reception in his own prayer-room at Littlemore, at the hands of a simple Italian priest on 9 October 1845, into the Roman Catholic Church.

It was almost exactly half-way through his life.

Intermezzo II

Interlude in Time

Filippo Neri –"of the trembling ecstasies"

Back to Rome now in this excursion (for which the reason will later become clear). Back three hundred years, to Renaissance Rome, to that Rome of the Council of Trent that had once so worried Newman, and that continued—indeed continues—to make Church of England evangelicals yelp, liberals shudder and Anglo-Catholics frown.

Nothing is more dangerous, history has shown again and again, than an unpaid army of mercenaries.[1] In those vast-ranging and fascinating wars for the control of Europe that raged between Francis I King of France and the great, the very Catholic King of Spain and Emperor, Charles V (with Henry VIII mainly tearing his beard on the sidelines) no single incident shocked Europe more than the *Sacco di Roma*, the Sack of Rome. The Imperial Army in the north of Italy, ferocious German *Landsknechte* most of them, unpaid for months, marched on Rome. The Constable of Bourbon, the commander, was killed in the assault on the walls. To the perpetual shame of his House, the Prince of Orange took over. The army stormed, sacked and for eight terrible days killed, tortured, raped, pillaged, destroyed and burnt the Eternal City.

Yet there was a consolation. As the great historian Burckhardt says, "Rome had suffered too much to return even under a Paul III to the gay corruption of Leo X." Serious men could once again make themselves heard.

Filippo Neri, a fourteen-year-old immigrant from Florence, was in one sense not a serious man at all. He had in him much of the spirit of Francis of Assisi. He was playful, a comedian, a joker, an eccentric; a holy man of sorts, but a very weird one. Yet in another sense he was a very serious figure indeed. Rather as Francis, with his love of Holy Poverty, had three centuries earlier reformed, or

---

1   See the present author's books on mercenaries, *passim*.

semi-reformed, the Church from the bottom up, so did Filippo Neri, with his own brand of holiness, lift Rome up from the ghastly, ruined, semi-obliterated state in which it found itself. Both had a characteristic, or perhaps a fortunate gift from above, in common. They both got on well with the popes of their day. The popes found them different, amusing. They tolerated them; they used them and finally they went on to reverence them; and indeed, pretty soon after their deaths, to canonize them.

Filippo's is a less dramatic story than Francis', if only because he stayed in one place for all his long, long life. He did not go on Crusade, like Francis, and confront the Saracens—the age of Crusades was over in any case. And though at one stage (inspired by that other St Francis, St Francis Xavier, of the newly-founded Society of Jesus) he wanted to go East as a missionary, he went to consult a very holy Cistercian monk, favoured with visions of St John, and was told, like the Delphic Oracle, to come back for an answer in a few days. Filippo went back. St John, it appears, had indeed appeared, and the somewhat disappointing response was "Rome is to be your Indies."

So, from the age of fifteen, Filippo stayed in Rome. He never went back once to Florence, though for his first eighteen years in Rome he lived as a kind of urban hermit, sleeping in a sparse little room in a fellow Florentine's house in Piazza di San Eustachio.

He wandered the streets, he prayed, he ate only olives and bread most days. He tried to study theology at the Sapienza briefly but then gave it up and sold his books. He walked out at night beyond the city walls and apparently would spend whole nights in the catacombs beneath the Appian Way.

It must have been an extraordinary life—an extraordinarily odd and aimless one. And then, when he was twenty-nine years old, at Pentecost, an even more extraordinary thing happened to him. He seemed to see a globe of fire which came down into his mouth and descended through his throat to his heart. Understandably enough, he felt as if he was on fire. Tearing his shirt off, he threw himself on the ground. When he rose, trembling violently but with an indescribable sense of joy, he found above his heart a swelling as big as a man's fist.

Was this a miracle? Was Filippo literally filled with the Holy Ghost? After his death they discovered that two of his ribs were broken and had thrust outwards and never knitted together again, that the main artery to his heart was twice the normal size, but that there were no signs of disease. For the rest of his life he would have violent palpitations of the heart, which sounded, according to his friends, like blows of a hammer, and go into trembling ecstasies, particularly when at prayer or at moments of high emotion. Certainly if Francis had the stigmata—which seems undeniable—why should not Filippo be visited by a similar, though considerably less painful, phenomenon?

Here I would like to quote Newman's views on miracles, which seem to me eminently sensible and are to be found in Note B to the *Apologia*. How far can they be applied to Filippo's seemingly miraculous visitation? Does it fulfil Newman's criteria? Let the reader decide…

> Catholics believe that miracles happen in any age of the Church, though not for the same purposes, in the same number, or with the same evidence, as in Apostolic times. On the report of a miracle they will, of necessity, the necessity of good logic, be led to say, first "It may be", and secondly, "But I must have good *evidence* in order to believe it."
>
> It may be, because miracles take place in all ages; it must be clearly *proved*, because perhaps after all it may only be a providential mercy, or an exaggeration, or a mistake, or an imposture.
>
> *What* has to be proved? (1) That the event occurred as stated and is not a false report or an exaggeration (2) That it is clearly miraculous, and not a mere providence or answer to prayer within the order of nature.

This seems admirably clear, and as miracles will feature in this age of the Church later in this book, and as the English, even English Catholics, are notoriously sceptical about miracles now as in Newman's day, I ask them to take a mental step back from their own prejudices and consider the logic of the position.

"In my *Essay on Miracles* of the year 1826," Newman continues, "I proposed three questions about a professed miraculous occurrence: (1) is it antecedently probable? (2) is it in its nature certainly miraculous? (3) has it sufficient evidence?" [Perhaps readers will apply these three questions with care and attention when it comes to—what Newman most certainly never envisaged—the miracle that led to Newman's own beatification.[2]]

Back to Filippo Neri. Just as Francis, after a weirdly solitary existence, starting doing good—in his case rebuilding a ruined little church outside Assisi—so Filippo began to do his bit, by visiting the sick in the great hospital of San Giacomo degli Incurabili. Not just visiting, either: sweeping the floors, washing people, changing them, praying with them too of course. But it was not till 1551, when he was aged thirty-six, that he finally became a priest and left his lodgings to install himself at the headquarters of a charitable archconfraternity in the little church of San Girolamo della Carita, just off the fashionable centre of Rome, the Via Giulia and the Campo di Fiori.

Here he found himself living directly opposite the English College on Via Monserrato, and legend has it that he would cheerily greet the young Jesuit seminarians every day with the encouraging cry of "good luck"—*Salvete*—"you picked bunch of martyrs"—*Flos Martyrum.*[3]

Legends gathered around Filippo, as indeed they had about Francis who, when attacked by bodily lust, used to go out, take off his clothes, and roll naked in the snow. A prostitute in Via Giulia, hearing that the new priest was so charming but yet so virtuous, decided to test him out. She asked him to come and hear her confession, and welcomed him wearing only a transparent veil. Filippo turned and ran. She threw a heavy wooden stool at him but missed. The moral of the tale, as Filippo was fond of telling his young disciples, was: when faced with temptations of the flesh, do not attempt to overcome them—just flee.

By now Filippo, with both a proper home and a proper job, was beginning to attract disciples. Obviously, like Francis, he had great

---

2 See pages 180-84. This bracketed section has been written by the present author in the Spring of 2010.
3 This, of course, was later on, in the 1570s, after the pope had installed Dr Allen and the English Jesuits.

charm—the charm of sanctity and sincerity as well as the charm of eccentricity.

Unlike Francis, he did not wish to found an order of any sort. There was no need of that—there were new orders galore in Rome— the Theatines, the Barnabites, the Jesuits—and he was friendly with all of them, often recommending young men to go off and join one or the other or the longer established Benedictines or Franciscans, or of course the Dominicans who had educated him as a boy at Fra Angelico's—and Fra Savonarola's—Convent of San Marco. But they clustered around him, and he was keen to keep them away from the temptations of idle young men in Rome, particularly in the long lazy afternoons, the most dangerous time of the day, he reckoned.

So every afternoon he would invite a group of them up to his room to read a holy book, and talk about it, and then perhaps go for a walk, and meet again in the evening for a prayer. As numbers expanded, he built a special room under the roof of San Girolamo that he called his Oratory, and gradually, inevitably, the meetings became less informal, more structured. Not too formal, though—one of his young men brought Cardinal Sforza's dog, Capriccio, over for a visit and Filippo virtually purloined it. Capriccio never left him till he (the dog, that is, not the cardinal) died. Another, a handsome young courtier, a future cardinal himself, by name of Tarugi, wanted to join the group but was entangled. Filippo foretold that the entanglement would end. It did. The lady in question died. A third, a young doctor, apparently dying of the stone, was cured after Filippo had visited him, then gone away and in one of his trembling ecstasies prayed for him.

Baronius, a very serious young man, described a typical afternoon session at the Oratory: first a reading on which Filippo commented, then a discussion, then three little talks. Baronius, who was to become famous as the first ecclesiastical historian, talked on Church history, and later claimed to have run through the whole history of the Church seven times over in twenty-seven years. A session lasted for about two hours. Then they sang a canticle, said a prayer; and that was it.

Except that the canticle—the singing and the music at the end—became more and more important. Special compositions

were specially written by, eventually, Palestrina himself.[4] Later on
the Florentines asked for the Oratory to be transferred to their own
Church of San Giovanni dei Fiorentini near the Ponte Sant Angelo.
A visitor wrote describing it all, very disarmingly, to his brother:

> There are three or four who preach everyday, and Bishops,
> prelates and other persons of distinction go to hear them. At
> the conclusion there is a little music to console and recreate
> the mind, which is fatigued by the preceding discourses.

Such were the beginnings of the Oratory. It had its troubles. At
one stage Filippo was hauled up before the pope's vicar—that was
in the time of the ferocious old reformer Paul IV—and accused
both of personal ambition and forming a sect. At another there
was, inevitably, the distressing departure of a splinter group. Filippo
himself continued to live at San Girolamo while his disciples were
installed in San Giovanni and trekked to and fro, three times a day.
Baronius at San Giovanni wrote above the fireplace *Baronius Coquus
Perpetuus*, a slightly self-mocking protest by the great writer of the
Annals at having to do all the cooking. Then there was a serious row,
calumnies, slanders, intrigue at San Giovanni—and finally in 1575,
to save the whole group, Pope Gregory XIII gave the Oratorians, as
they were beginning to be called, not only a Constitution (they were
to be, in perpetuity, "a Congregation of secular priests and clerics
known as the Oratory") but also, at last, a little church of their own,
Santa Maria in Vallicella.

Filippo was in his late fifties now. Rather surprisingly, late in
life, he got bitten by the building bug. Santa Maria in Vallicella was
small, dark, and half ruined. Filippo decided to demolish it and
build on its site a splendid New Church, the Chiesa Nuova. Carlo
Borromeo, the Archbishop of Milan, who in a sense was to Milan

---

4   And hence is derived the musical term Oratorio, to be used, eventually, even by
Lutherans like Handel.

what Filippo Neri was to Rome,[5] gave 400 crowns, and the pope contributed a lavish 8000 crowns. The new congregation bought the neighbouring monastery of St Elizabeth as living quarters, and finally a reluctant Filippo was given a direct order, in 1578, by the pope to leave his beloved perch at San Girolamo and come and live with his congregation in their splendid new abode.

He obeyed and became the *Preposito*, the Provost. But even then, he lived a rather separate life in a remote room, with a loggia on the roof where he could pray by himself beneath the sky. One thing he did, however, absolutely insist on: that the new congregation should be different from the other Religious Orders, in fact should not be, formally speaking, a Religious Order at all.

The defining feature of religious communities was that their members took vows. Filippo was not having that. No vows, ever. The Oratory was to be a free association of like-minded priests living together—clearly with certain rules, but everyone was to be free to own private property (no vow of poverty) and keep it if they wished—though it would be more natural to contribute more if one were richer. And everyone was free to leave at any time if they wished (no vow of stability). Filippo was so determined on this that he ruled that if after his death a majority of the Oratorians should wish to change the system, it would have to be the majority who departed—and the vowless minority, however small, would retain both the property and the title of the Congregation.

Not that he wanted there to be much property. He was against the Oratory expanding. When the persuasive Carlo Borromeo pressingly, again and again, urged him to send at least a group to Milan—the greatest city in Europe at the time—he hesitated, then refused. Yet the general idea of the Oratory was too attractive not to be imitated. Tarugi went to Naples for his health, on a visit, and the Neapolitans so enjoyed the informal style of his sermons that they forced him to

---

5 Carlo Borromeo, an aristocrat born in 1538, was the most successful example of nepotism in the Renaissance Church. Created a cardinal by his uncle Pope Pius IV, he led a short, adventurous, highly political but reforming, holy and charitable life. He founded the Oblates of St Ambrose, later to be taken as an example to be imitated by the future Cardinal Manning. He died in 1584, was canonised (not by his uncle) and is known in English as St Charles Borromeo.

stay. Filippo agreed, finally, to an Oratory being formed in Naples too, and sent four or five more down to join Tarugi. But it was always a worry to him, this outlying branch. And eventually, after his death it became a principle that each and every congregation of the Oratory should be self-governing. There was, and is, no centralised control—totally, of course, unlike the Jesuits or indeed the Dominicans.

Filippo was often ill in those years at the Chiesa Nuova, often apparently near death, but again and again he recovered. There is one quite remarkable story of a miracle in his old age—there are countless others of cures, answers to prayers, sudden conversions, almost as many as grew up around Francis of Assisi—but this is the only one that is, in the right sense, legendary. It involved a death—and a resurrection.

One of Filippo's friends was Fabrizio de' Massimi. On 16 March 1583 Filippo was saying Mass when he was summoned to come urgently to the Palazzo Massimi. Fabrizio's fourteen-year-old son, Paolo, was on the point of death. Filippo had been visiting the boy regularly. But when he arrived half an hour later Paolo was dead—and already being prepared for burial. Fabrizio, his wife and a maid were in the room and witnessed what happened next.

Filippo, trembling, with palpitations, prayed by the boy's body for a few minutes. He then sprinkled the body with holy water, laid his hands on the boy's forehead and called him twice by name: "Paolo! Paolo!"

Paolo opened his eyes and began talking. He and Filippo chatted for a quarter of an hour. Filippo asked him if he was ready now to go to Heaven. He replied in a clear voice. He said that he was. Then he died again.

An extraordinary miracle; and in a way a miracle that makes no sense. The father and the mother were absolutely convinced that Paolo was dead, well and truly dead in the first place, and that he had been brought to life again for a quarter of an hour by Filippo Neri. They converted the room where this had happened into a chapel; and still, every year, on 16 March, the "feast of the miracle" is specially celebrated there in Rome.

At confessions Filippo seemed to know what sins the penitents should confess; and when they failed to do so, filled in the gaps for them. When he was dying—a favourite saying of his was "Last of all we must die"—he seemed to be able to foretell the exact hour of his death. "Three and two are five, three and three are six, and then I shall go." But he was never gloomy: "I will have no low spirits, no melancholy in my house," he used to say. When he one day found a depressed priest, his method of cure was unusual: "Come now, let us run together." "Paradise," he used to say, "is no place for sluggards." More seriously: "The man without prayer is like an animal without reason." And the four steps toward holiness are, "To despise the world, to despise no man, to despise oneself, and to despise being despised." That is a saying that needs thinking about.

Gregory XIV tried to create him a cardinal. Filippo treated it as a joke. Clement VIII wanted Filippo as his personal confessor, but was turned down. Filippo once summoned Clement to see him. "As to going to see you," the pope replied, "the Pope says that Your Reverence does not deserve it since you will not accept the cardinalate so many times offered you."

Filippo Neri died, in his own room surrounded by the Fathers of the Oratory, peacefully enough and at the hour foretold, on 26 May 1595. He was aged almost eighty. Immediately there were cries for him to be proclaimed a saint (and reports of visions of him in glory, miracles obtained by touching his body, and so forth). He was beatified—declared Blessed—twenty years later; and on 12 March 1522, less than thirty years after his death, the Romans complained that the pope had canonized that morning in St Peter's "four Spaniards and one Saint"![6]

He was the Saint. In English he is known as St Philip Neri; and in Rome, *pace* St Peter, as the "Apostle of Rome".

---

6 Three of the four Spaniards are better known than Filippo Neri. They were St Ignatius Loyola, founder of the Jesuits, his contemporary and follower, St Francis Xavier, the Apostle of the Indies and that extraordinary woman of the world and nun, St Teresa of Avila.

Chapter Four

The Convert - and Four Crises

Pio Nono – the pope of the "Papal Aggression"

"I stagger to and fro like a drunken man. I am at my wit's end." The news of Newman's conversion caused immense shock and grief—this reaction, typical enough, was Gladstone's, writing to Archdeacon Manning.

And it was not just Newman. Shortly before, W.G. Ward resigned his fellowship, married and converted, and with his conversion the Oxford Movement effectively came to an end. Shortly after, there was George Ryder, Manning's brother-in-law. He took his three children and his sister Sophy abroad, and in Naples they all converted. Much to Jemima Newman's disgust—she disapproved of it all, thoroughly, consistently, her brother's "betrayal" most of all—Sophia, the young Mrs Ryder, youngest of the beautiful Miss Sargents, loyally followed her rash husband. Rash, because the Reverend George had, of course, to resign his living. He and his young family were penniless, homeless, ostracised by family, friends, society in general.

Even the iron-clad Gladstone seems, for a moment, to have been tempted. That autumn—he was out of office at the time, very temporarily though; he rejoined Peel's government as Secretary of State for the Colonies when he got back—he spent two months in Germany. On Hope-Scott's urging in Munich he called on a famous German theologian (and Catholic priest) Dr Döllinger. German scholarship was a source of wonder and admiration in England at the time—immensely erudite, immensely serious. "I spent a good deal of time in Dr Döllinger's company last night till one o'clock. He seemed to me one of the most liberal and catholic of all the persons of his communion I have known. I have quite lost my heart to him," wrote Gladstone to his wife.

But it was a visit to a group of Catholic ladies in Baden-Baden a little later that seems really to have shaken him. "I have drunk tea several times and have had two or three long conversations with them on matters of religion. They are excessively acute and also full of

Christian sentiment. But they are much more difficult to make real way with than a professor of theology, because they are determined (what is vulgarly called) to go the whole hog."

It does sound as if the great parliamentarian had lost the argument, and was only too aware of it.

Back in England there were indeed hopes that even the mighty Gladstone might come over. Wiseman was back in England permanently now, installed as President of Oscott, the Catholic seminary and college outside Birmingham, full of enthusiasm for the conversion of England. His old pupil, Father George Spencer, had been installed as spiritual director at Oscott, and Spencer had persuaded the Archbishop of Paris and the French Provincial of the Jesuits to launch a crusade of prayer for the conversion of England throughout France. Wiseman, now a bishop, with all his impulsive enthusiasm had taken up the cause.

"Let us have an influx of new blood," he wrote to Ambrose Phillipps, "let us have but even a small number of men such as write in the Tracts—let even a few such men, with the high clerical spirit which I believe them to possess, enter fully into the spirit of the Catholic Religion and *we* shall be speedily reformed and England quickly converted."

This was not at all to the taste of the Vicars Apostolic and the Catholic clergy in general. Apart from the incoming Italians, with their extravagant devotions, they and the Old Catholics were all for a low profile and a quiet life. Ambrose Phillipps, however, was in close contact with many men in Oxford: W.G. Ward, Frederick Faber and, in particular, the Reverend Bloxam, Newman's great friend. What he most desired, he wrote to Bloxam, was "a good understanding between the Catholic and the Anglican Church, with a view to the ultimate restoration of that happy and blessed Unity which formerly existed between them for more than a thousand years". Wishful thinking then, wishful thinking now. But Ambrose Phillipps believed it utterly, Father Spencer believed it—both of them, and Wiseman too, Wiseman perhaps most of all. For he remembered as a red-letter day the visit that Newman and Hurrell Froude had paid him in Rome at the English College, and he was convinced that if Newman came over, once Newman came over, the rectors and vicars and curates and the laity, even perhaps the bishops and archbishops of the Church of England, would follow Newman's lead *en masse*. He expected the total conversion of England.

Yet in 1842 Wiseman had had a shock. A young Fellow of Magdalen, a colleague therefore of Bloxam's, by name Sibthorpe, came to Oscott, was wildly impressed, converted, was swiftly ordained priest, sent to Pugin's St Chad, as swiftly became disillusioned with Birmingham as compared to Oxford, reneged, relapsed, apostatised and rejoined the Anglican Church.

Wiseman, as he often did in moments of depression, took to his bed for several days and nights. The Old Catholics, somewhat smugly but rather rightly, pointed out the dangers of too hasty conversions.

Which, of course, was not the case with Newman. Newman had always kept Wiseman, and Spencer, and indeed all the Catholic clergy and laymen too at arm's length while he had pondered his path. There had been correspondence but in guarded terms. When Newman finally made his move, no-one could accuse him of having acted *à la* Sibthorpe—hastily and impulsively.

Newman left Littlemore without regrets. He had a last evening with old friends in Oxford; and then "Mr Newman's Cottages" emptied. On 31 October, hand held by Father Spencer, he arrived at Oscott and the next day, the Feast of All Saints, was confirmed by its President, Bishop Wiseman.

It must have been an odd meeting for both of them. Newman was understandably shy—he was being thrown into a totally new, almost alien environment. Physically Wiseman had changed from the tall thin rector Newman had met over twelve years ago at the English College. Wiseman was still tall, of course, over six foot two, but he had become gross: "a ruddy-faced and somewhat corpulent man of action," W.G. Ward described him as; or, as Frederick Faber rather more disrespectfully put it: "when in full tog he looked like some Japanese God." But children adored him. Even the future Lord Acton, a priggish schoolboy at Oscott, said later that "we were proud of him, we were not afraid of him. He was approachable and gracious and no great friend to discipline." "Once I was told that he was ugly," another pupil was to write, "and I could not believe it. He was so delightful to us that I could not fancy that he was anything but handsome." He was a warm-hearted, enthusiastic, generous man, a *bon viveur*, with fascinating stories, capable of lecturing on science and literature as much as on religion, slightly pompous with other clerics—he had, after all, lived in Roman society most of his life—but utterly relaxed, arm in arm, with such visitors to Oscott as Daniel O'Connell, the Liberator.

All in all, he was not, and never would be, Newman's kindred spirit. But, though their first meeting was awkward and conversation stilted and, to the relief of both men, soon ended, the bishop treated Newman with surprising delicacy and tact. He immediately offered him and his disciples—for none of them could bear the thought of being separated from their guide, philosopher and friend and, of course, their futures were extremely obscure—a home, and a very spacious one, in the buildings of Old Oscott. For Oscott itself by now had moved into Pugin's new buildings.

Wiseman suggested that the new converts should go to Rome for a course of study—a very wise suggestion, one that would make them, once back from Rome, much more welcome, given the pope's seal of approval, among the suspicious Old Catholics. But first Wiseman proposed that they should make a round of visits and meet their fellow Catholics. Thus, wrote Wiseman to Dr Russell of Maynooth, the great Irish seminary, Newman "will soon be known to all the clergy, and popular among them." Optimistic indeed.

Newman started well. At St Edmund's Ware he struck up an instant friendship with Robert Whitty, "a more winning person I have not met, though an Irishman," he wrote to St John. In London he pretty nearly forced Maria Giberne to see Father Brownbill at Farm Street. "The terrible Jesuit," she called him. "Do you think Mr Brownbill a clever and deeply learned man? I do not. I shall never get accustomed to anyone but you." She converted all the same, made her confession into Brownbill's "large red ear", and soon enough was urging all her friends to follow her example.[1]

Not quite so successful was a visit to Alton Towers. There Newman found himself understandably ill-at-ease, in his own words "feeling like a fool". It was "a house full of company", and a grander house, by far, than any Newman had ever stayed in before. Lord and Lady Camoys were there, Lord and Lady Dormer, Sir Robert Throckmorton, Sir Edward Vavasour, ambassadors and bishops aplenty, and Newman had the feeling of being a sort of prize exhibit, displayed for show. But the good Earl[2] was "most kind"; and though Ambrose Phillipps with his mediaeval passions was by no means Newman's type of fellow convert, Newman had the satisfaction of learning that George Ryder and his young family (which included Newman's godson, little Lisle) had in their forsaken state been given a home by their cousin, on the Grace Dieu estate.

On 7 September Newman and the other Ambrose, Ambrose St John, crossed the Channel to Dieppe on their way to Rome. En route Newman, quite a celebrity in Europe, was fêted. In Rome, they were comfortably lodged at the College of Propaganda, and soon enough summoned to the Vatican to meet the new pope.

Pio Nono, as he was popularly called, Pope Pius IX, was warm and friendly, open-hearted, and at this stage open-minded and liberal too. He was to preside over the fortunes of the Church for the next thirty-one years, the longest pontificate ever; and he was the first pope so popular, so widely known and instantly recognised that his portrait was to be found in almost every Catholic household. Newman found him "Easy and affable", and he joked with Ambrose St John, who had already learnt a little Italian.

One of Newman's failings was that he had no ability to learn new languages. He did not speak or read German—which barred him

---

1 I do not think Mrs Bowden was a friend of Miss Giberne. But she and her family followed soon afterwards in any case; as did Emily Bowles.

2 Alton Towers came to a sad ending. The good Earl, the 16th earl, died in Naples in 1852. His cousin the 17th earl, Earl Bertram, died aged only 24 four years later. The title and the fortune eventually passed after a series of ruinous lawsuits to a remote non-Catholic branch of the family who had no interest in maintaining the traditions of their House. In 1990 Madame Tussaud's bought the ruin of Alton Towers and it is now an amusement park. The present earl, the 22nd, lives, I believe, in Switzerland.

from the most up-to-date theological studies—and he never properly learnt Italian. He was, after all, forty-five, whereas most of the other students at Propaganda—and thirty-two nationalities were there—were much younger men. Fortunately the official language in Rome, the language of study, was Latin. But his inability to learn the *lingua franca* certainly was a hindrance. Nevertheless, for a much older man in a very strange environment he adapted pretty well.

The main question was: what was to be Newman's future? And it seems almost to have been assumed, as a matter of course, that he, the former vicar, would be ordained a priest. There was no obstacle of wife and family. There were worries in some quarters in the Vatican about the *Essay*. Were his theories on the Development of Christian Doctrine not verging, in parts, on heresy? The worries passed. He and St John were both ordained in the Church at Propaganda by Cardinal Fransoni.

That was on Trinity Sunday, 1 June 1847, only a year and a half after having arrived in Rome. In the meantime the great dilemma had had to be decided: should they be secular priests, ordinary clergy, or should they join an order? And if so, what order?

"From what I have heard of the Dominican ethos," Ambrose St John wrote to Dalgairns (who had already been ordained a priest in France), "they put me in mind of the old Anglican high and dry's. The Jesuits, be my calling what it may, are a wonderful body. The Passionists have a high name—too strict though for poor dear old human nature. The Redemptorists have no house here but they have a very high character indeed as a rising order. Their great house is in Naples, and see them we certainly ought." As for Newman himself, he had ideas of founding a college of theology in England. Dalgairns was rather for joining the Dominicans whatever Ambrose St John might feel. Newman remained judicious. "There is no doubt that the Jesuits are the *only* persons here," he wrote to Dalgairns. "They say however that the Dominicans are rising in Italy. You shall come and judge for yourself. You have plenty of cash."

We have seen the *Chiesa Nuova* and the *Casa* adjoining, the small room where St Philip had his ecstasies. The *Casa* is the most beautiful thing we have seen in Rome—rather too comfortable i.e. fine galleries for walking in summer, splendid orange trees etc etc.

If I wished to follow my bent, I should join the Oratorians. They have a good library and handsome sets of rooms apparently. It is like a College with hardly any rule. They keep their own property, and furnish their own rooms.

It is what Dr Wiseman actually wishes, and really I should not wonder if at last I felt strongly inclined to it, for I must own I feel the notion of giving up property tries my faith very much.

And so, for these very English reasons, it was decided. Not only Wiseman approved, the pope approved. He had Newman summon all his disciples to Rome—Dalgairns, Bowles and Stanton, and two more, Coffin and Penny—installed them all at the monastery of Santa Croce, and appointed an Italian Oratorian to be their Novice Master, to show them the ropes. Newman was excited—the English Oratory must be *located* in a *town,* he emphasised—and not all Italian customs could be followed. Baronius would serve as an example; plenty of time there must be for study and books. But just as Baronius had served the hospitals, so he too would much prefer a season of *active duty* before returning to his books. London? Birmingham? And what of Old Oscott, which Newman, echoing Santa Maria in Vallicella, had renamed Maryvale? Maybe Birmingham to start with, the *Oratorio* open from October to June, and then the summer months outside the city, with the Confraternity marching out on holy days to Maryvale?

Newman made great friends with the new Secretary of Propaganda, Monsignore Palma, who prepared a brief for the English Oratory. They visited the Oratorians at Naples, most of whom were "young lively pleasant persons", and Newman, relaxed, happy, in high spirits, did a very odd thing for Newman. He wrote a novel.

Loss and Gain, like most first novels, is very autobiographical, as its sub-title, *The Story of a Convert*, might suggest. The hero, Charles Reding, is not, however, one of a brood of six but the only son of a clergyman. There is Oxford; and "About 3 miles from Oxford is the thickly-wooded village" of New Common; and the hero ends up, at the grand finale, "kissing Father Aloysius' hand". It is not the greatest novel in the world. But it did run to fourteen editions by the end of the century, and on occasions Newman let his satirical pen run nicely wild. Compared to the *Apologia*—not yet, of course, so much as dreamt of—it is a lighter way of studying his conversion.

On the journey back to England Newman and St John, now his fellow priest, had tea with the great Dr Döllinger in Munich, and on Christmas Eve 1847 Father Newman celebrated his first Mass in England in the private chapel Mrs Bowden had fitted out in her house in Chelsea. Newman's godson, little Charles Bowden, was his altar boy.

All seemed set fair, troubles over, the future settled, free of anguish and dilemmas, easy, rosy.

It was not to be. The rule of the Catholic Church is that no man, or woman, can become a saint in heaven unless in this life on earth they have shown "heroic virtue". And in the years to come, I would argue, with all the stresses and strains and crises he was due to face, Newman did indeed show heroic patience, heroic tact, and a potpourri of heroic virtues.

Not at first, perhaps. At first there were the inevitable teething troubles that beset the founding of any new organisation, and particularly an organisation like the Oratory that depended not on rules and regulations and a well-ordered hierarchy but on the harmonious living together of like-minded men. Newman had to spend a great deal of the rest of his life, and energy, placating, urging, encouraging, soothing ruffled feelings (including his own), and holding his little community together; and he did not always succeed. He sometimes felt that no one, except the ever-loyal and hard-working Ambrose St John, was supporting him. He particularly missed his family. But one of his brothers, Charles, was the black sheep; Frank had veered away into extreme views, and his two married sisters, Jemima and Harriet, on whom he had so relied, would hardly have anything at all to do with their eldest brother now that he had "betrayed" the Church of

England, to which for all the rest of their lives they, and their Mozley husbands, remained unshakeably attached.

The first trouble arose with Frederick Faber and his followers. Faber was a much younger man, just in his thirties—Harrow, Balliol, a supporter at Balliol of the Oxford Movement, Fellow of University College, ordained into the Church of England, then for three years Rector of Elton in Huntingdonshire. Faber had "come over" almost simultaneously with Newman, and, much to Wiseman's delight, he had brought a whole batch of young men with him. Lord Shrewsbury, with his usual generosity, had offered Faber and his group a country house near Stoke, Cotton Hall, which Faber transferred into "St Wilfred's" and his group of seventeen eager young converts into "Wilfridians". No sooner was Newman back in Maryvale than Bishop Wiseman informed him that the Wilfridians, *en masse*, wanted to join his new Oratory.

Here is not the place to go into all the difficulties and rows and scenes that followed. Faber and Newman never really got on, the Wilfridians "swarmed" over the original Oratorians, the good Earl became the angry Earl, understandably enough, when there was talk of abandoning Cotton Hall where Pugin had added a church; and Ambrose Phillipps had a famous stand-up row with Faber over gothic versus classical church furnishings. "God will curse and destroy your Order and it will perish if you go on thus," the irate Squire of Grace Dieu, waving his fists, declaimed.

Newman calmed them down, and the new Vicar Apostolic of the Central District, Bishop Ullathorne, a plain blunt traditional Yorkshireman who had been a cabin-boy, a minister to the convicts in Australia and a Benedictine monk at Downside, calmed everyone down—all these new nervy converts, a mixed blessing, he no doubt thought. The upshot was that there was one Oratory in Birmingham, in Alcester Street, a converted gin distillery, opened on 26 January 1849 with Newman as Superior; and another Oratory in London, a gin shop, at King William Street off the Strand, of which Faber, twenty months later, became the Superior. As for Cotton Hall, Newman thought that eventually it might become a school—in fact it was to be sold to the Passionists.

The dust settled. But it had not been without its cost. Whitty, the Irishman whom Newman had met at St Edmund's Ware and found so delightful, joined the Oratory in Birmingham, but his real desire was to work among the Irish poor in London, vast numbers of whom were settling in the docklands after fleeing the Famine. But Whitty could not stand Faber. So he left the Oratory and eventually became the right-hand-man of Wiseman, who had been shifted to London as Vicar Apostolic of the London District. Coffin left too; he could not bear Faber either, and that was the loss of another priest of talent, for he joined the Redemptorists and was eventually to become their Provincial and, later, Bishop of Southwark.

On the other hand, right from the start the Oratory in Birmingham attracted vast crowds, as the Irish were flooding into Birmingham too, and the face of English Catholicism (and its numbers) was changing for ever.[3] Congregations spilled out of the church onto the pavements and the neighbouring streets, and parish work in which Newman, though the Superior, took an equal part consumed the time and energies of the now rather sparsely staffed Birmingham Oratory.

But whatever teething troubles afflicted the nascent Oratory, they were as nothing to the woes that descended first on the pope in Rome, then on the Anglican Church, and thirdly on the Catholics in England in general.

In the autumn of 1848 the pope was driven by armed force from Rome. Not the mercenaries of Spain this time, but the Italian nationalists: Mazzini, Garibaldi and *Casa Savoia*. There was no Sack but it was not bloodless. Pio Nono's prime minister, Count Rossi, was murdered and Newman's great friend and supporter at Propaganda, Monsignore Palma, was shot and killed at a window in the Quirinal Palace. The pope fled to Gaeta, the Republic was proclaimed. A year later French troops under General Oudinot restored the papacy. But that year of revolution had completely changed Pio Nono's outlook. From an easy-going and moderate liberal, a reformer, he became a

---

3 Up to totals of between 600,000 and 680,000 by 1850, over three per cent of the population.

fierce political reactionary. One can understand why. But thus he lost the sympathy of the English Liberals—of Palmerston, of Lord John Russell, of Gladstone (not yet a Liberal, but veering that way) and of all who supported the movement for Italian unity and loathed not so much papal rule in the Papal States as the Bourbon regime in the south, where Ferdinand II, second (and penultimate) King of the Two Sicilies, Gladstone's bugbear-to-be, King "Bomba" to the rest of Europe, shelled his own towns to put down the revolution.

But at the time, closer to home, Gladstone and his friends had other worries: the Gorham Judgment. "This stupendous issue," Gladstone called it. It had all begun in December 1847. The Reverend George Gorham, a combative clergyman, was unsound on Baptismal Regeneration. His even more combative bishop, Philpotts, the Bishop of Exeter, had him examined for seven days, after which he refused to install him. The Reverend Gorham appealed to the Court of Arches. The Court of Arches, an ecclesiastical court, supported the bishop against the clergyman. Whereupon Gorham went one step further and appealed from the Court of Arches to the Judicial Committee of the Privy Council.

The "stupendous issue" was not so much Baptismal Regeneration, right or wrong, yes or no, in itself (though indeed that tended to split the Church of England) as this: was it right, was it fitting, was it admissible, for a court of laymen like the Law Lords of the Judicial Committee to decide, one way or another, on what the doctrine of the Church of England should or should not be? For two years it was a burning question. And finally, on 8 March 1850, the Judicial Committee gave its long-awaited judgement. The Court of Arches' decision was reversed. In effect the state had the power to decide what the Church should or should not believe. Gladstone was ill in bed in Carlton Terrace when judgement was delivered. Manning, who was in London, went to see him. Gladstone sat up, threw up his arms. "The Church of England is gone!" he exclaimed.

A meeting followed at St Paul's, Knightsbridge. Archdeacon Manning was asked to preside. Gladstone was there, Hope-Scott too, Keble and Pusey, and many others. The proposition at length accepted by all was: "if the Church of England shall accept this Judgement it would forfeit its authority as a divine teacher." Hope-Scott ruined the harmony by interjecting, "I suppose we are all agreed that if the Church of England does not undo this we must join the Church of Rome?" All agreed they most certainly were not. Later Gladstone was to mutter to Manning: "Do you think that I as a Privy Councillor should sign this Declaration?" Manning did not press the point; and Gladstone did not sign.

It was at this stage that Newman took a hand. He decided to come up and deliver a series of public lectures at the London Oratory in King William Street. This was in its way both sensational news and a social occasion. For here would be Newman, of whom almost nothing had been heard for five years, who had been out of circulation for longer even than that, the famous silver-tongued preacher of the University Church, stepping back into the public gaze—and this time as Father Newman, the Popish priest!

It is an exaggeration to say that all London flocked to King William Street. But the lectures were very, very popular. There were twelve in all, delivered every Monday from 9 May onwards and entitled *Lectures on Certain Difficulties felt by Anglicans in submitting to the Catholic Church*. Newman was in a happy, optimistic frame of mind—glad to be back in London, at ease even with Father Faber (who, with Wiseman, was usually in the audience—though of course it was not to them that the lectures were addressed) and happy too about the Birmingham Oratory which a surprising £10,000 legacy would enable to move—the new site was bought that very month of May—from the Alcester Street gin distillery out to Edgbaston and then, eventually, into its own community house with "funds too for an attached church".

Brilliant and stimulating and frank as the lectures were—they were soon to be published, following Newman's usual practice, in book form—they did not rope in a new herd of converts, as intended. Instead, the spotlight was now to shift, violently, away from the difficulties of the Anglican Church and onto the evil intentions, the wicked designs, the intolerable presumption, of Rome.

Wiseman always had in him something of the child. He was overjoyed when he was summoned to Rome and told he was going to be appointed a Prince of the Church, a cardinal, (for Cardinal Acton, the almost obligatory English cardinal, had died at the age of only 45) but burst into tears when it hit him that he would have to abandon his work on the spot for the conversion of England and live in Rome for the rest of his life.

In fact that was not the pope's plan at all. The idea was to abolish all the Vicars Apostolic, declare England no longer missionary territory, take it away gradually from under the wing of Propaganda and set up a proper hierarchy, with bishops and archbishops, dioceses and an archdiocese just as if it were Spain or France. And Wiseman was to be the new archbishop—not, of course, of Canterbury since that would have been going too far seeing that there was already an Archbishop of Canterbury and indeed an Archbishop of York. But why not of, for instance, Westminster?

On 29 September Pio Nono's Brief re-establishing the hierarchy was proclaimed, and the same day Wiseman was named Archbishop of Westminster. On the following day a Consistory was held; and he became Cardinal Wiseman, taking the oath in the Sistine Chapel, lying prostrate on the floor while the *Te Deum* was sung.

The Times was not amused. "If this appointment be not intended as a clumsy joke," thundered the Thunderer, "we confess that we can only regard it as one of the grossest acts of folly and impertinence which the Court of Rome has ventured to commit since the Crown and people of England threw off its yoke." Priests and their congregations were hooted. A new and damning phrase became current—the Papal Aggression.

In Rome, knowing nothing of this, enjoying it all, the new cardinal took the fatal step which changed what might just have been a nine-day-wonder into, almost (though not quite), rioting in the streets. In his ebullience he issued a Pastoral.

"Nicholas," it began, "by the Divine mercy, of the Holy Roman Church of St Pudentiana Cardinal Priest, Archbishop of Westminster, and Administrator Apostolic of the Diocese of Southwark. To our dearly beloved in Christ, the Clergy secular and regular, and the faithful of the said Archdiocese and Diocese, Health and Benediction in the Lord!" Thanking His Holiness for appointing him archbishop he added, a touch bombastically, "so that at present and till such time as the Holy See shall think otherwise to provide, we govern and shall continue to govern, the Counties of Middlesex, Hertford and Essex as ordinary thereof, and those of Surrey, Sussex, Kent, Berkshire and Hampshire with the islands annexed, as administrator with ordinary jurisdiction."

This was the passage that had Queen Victoria, when she read it, spluttering over her soup. She was not amused. "Am I Queen of England or am I not?" she, understandably, furiously, asked.

Wiseman rounded off his Pastoral with the phrase that occasioned most mockery of all: "Given out of the Flaminian Gate of Rome, this seventh day of October in the year of Our Lord MDCCCL."

Unaware of the brewing hurricane, having sent his Pastoral ahead with orders that it be read out to the rejoicing faithful from every Catholic pulpit in England, the new cardinal travelled back towards England with the pomp that befitted his new office.

The wretched Whitty, back in London, hardly knew whether to censor the inflammatory Pastoral or send it out. In the end he felt he could hardly disobey Wiseman's direct written instructions. On Sunday 27 October it was indeed read out, and fury erupted all over England. Usurping "an imaginary see of Westminster" was the least of it. "We are not aware," the editor of *The Times* held, "that the misuse of language ever reached a more frightful perversion."

Wiseman was lunching with the emperor in Vienna when he first heard of the furore. That was on 1 November. Quite courageously he decided to hurry back to England and face the music in person. On 4 November the prime minister, Lord John Russell, wrote a vehement letter to the Bishop of Durham condemning utterly the pope and all his works and deeds and promising drastic vengeful action.[4] On 5 November, Guy Fawkes Day, effigies of Pio Nono in his Papal Triple Crown were burnt all over England; and of Cardinal

---

4 Not entirely surprising. The Russell family owed its lands, vast fortune and titles to the success of Sir John Russell in helping to crush the Pilgrimage of Grace in 1536 in Henry VIII's time and in utterly crushing the Prayer Book Rebellion in 1549 in Edward VI's time. The Bedfords were therefore always rabidly anti-Catholic.

Wiseman too, dressed up here as a Papal Bull with horns, there as a braying donkey with flapping ears. The ancient war cry of Protestant England—"No Popery!"—was chanted again throughout our green and pleasant land. There were innumerable meetings of protest. The Lord Chancellor himself proclaimed, amidst wild applause: "Under our feet we'll stamp the Cardinal's hat."

Unexpectedly it was Wiseman himself, back in London at Southwark, who plastered his own wound. He produced, within a fortnight, a 32-page pamphlet entitled *An Appeal to the Reason and Good Feeling of the English People.*

"There still remains," he wrote, with the bombast of his Pastoral completely cast aside, "the manly sense and honest heart of a generous people; that love of honourable dealing and fair play which, in joke or in earnest, is equally the instinct of an Englishman. To this open-fronted and warm-hearted tribunal I make my appeal, and claim, on behalf of myself and my fellow Catholics, a free, fair and impartial hearing."[5]

The new dioceses created, besides the archdiocese of Westminster, were Beverley, Birmingham, Clifton, Hexham and Newcastle, Liverpool, Newport and Menevia in Wales, Northampton, Nottingham, Plymouth, Salford, Shrewsbury of course, Southampton and Plymouth. So there were twelve Catholic bishops, mainly in towns and cities where poor Irish labourers were living in large numbers; and the titles, carefully enough, rarely if ever clashed with those of existing Anglican bishoprics.

Gradually the English came to accept that it was simply an administrative measure, and by early December Lord John Russell was receiving a message from the Palace that announced: "The Queen deeply regrets the great abuse of the Roman Catholic religion which takes place at all these meetings etc. She thinks it unchristian and unwise, and trusts that it will soon cease."

---

5 An appeal that the present Archbishop of Westminster might consider repeating in view of the present flurry of anti-pope agitation. But would the papers, nowadays, ever agree to publish a 32-page refutation in full? As, to their credit, *The Times*, and other newspapers, did on 21 November. The editor, a little reluctantly, added: "We congratulate Dr Wiseman on his recovery of the use of the English language."

It did, though Lord John Russell proceeded with the Ecclesiastical Titles Bill, outlawing the new titles. It passed into law but was never enforced. And, twenty years later, Mr Gladstone as prime minister repealed it.

But the phrase "Out of the Flaminian Gate" long stuck in the craw of the English people and remained to haunt Wiseman all his life.

Before all this, two things had happened that year. First Wiseman, still in England, still a comparatively humble cleric, had written a long article in the *Dublin Review* condemning the activities of a defrocked Dominican, Achilli by name, who had come to England and was wooing admiring audiences (that increased enormously of course during the autumn crisis) by attacking his former Church. Wiseman had learnt that he, Achilli, had seduced young women, and sometimes children, all over Italy and was in fact a thoroughly nasty piece of work. And he published what he knew. From Mr Achilli there was no reaction at all at the time.

That was in June 1850. That same month a Bill designed to make it impossible for the Judicial Committee of the Privy Council ever again to lay down what was or what was not the correct teachings of the Anglican Church—in other words a Bill to keep the state out of matters that, obviously, should be the Church's concern alone, to prevent any future Gorham Judgement—was rejected by the House of Lords.

For Manning this was to be the final straw. He went up to Abbotsford in the winter. And on 5 April 1851, having resigned his living and his position as Archdeacon of Chichester, both he and Hope-Scott were received into the Catholic Church by Father Brownbill, the red-eared Jesuit of Farm Street. That left, of all the four clergymen who had married the four beautiful Miss Sargents, only "Soapy Sam" still in orders in the Church of England.

And that left Gladstone deprived, at one blow, of his two best friends, the two godfathers of his eldest son. "They were my twin props," he noted the next day in his diary. But "these dismal events have smitten, not shaken". It was the end of his friendship with the ex-archdeacon. The two men formally returned to each other the letters they had over the years exchanged. As for Hope-Scott, a barrister (in fact now a QC) his "treachery" was clearly not as great as an ordained minister's. "Yours with unaltered affection," Gladstone wrote to him. But he immediately removed Hope-Scott as executor of his will.

Shortly before, Henry Wilberforce and his wife and family had at last converted. Newman had been writing to Henry for five years long, detached, urging letters—that was his way, no attempt at mass conversions but every attempt to convert, to save the souls and make use of the intellect of his dear friends, individually, by personal persuasion.

Not quite true, of course. The lectures in King William Street in London had been an attempt, of sorts, at a mass conversion of his Anglican friends and admirers, ruined in that case by the kerfuffle (that came only too hard on the heels of the lectures) of the Papal Aggression.

Totally different were the lectures that Newman delivered at the Corn Exchange in Birmingham after the kerfuffle had died down. They were addressed to Catholics, not Anglicans (in theory to "my fellow priests of the Oratory in Birmingham") but in fact the audience included, besides Bishop Ullathorne, now Bishop of Birmingham, both the "new" converts and brothers-in-law, Manning and Henry Wilberforce.

The title of these lectures was *On the Present position of Catholics in England*, there were nine of them, and they were delivered once a week from the end of June to the beginning of September 1851 and almost immediately, as usual, published in book form—another 400 pages or so.

They were great fun. They enlivened the dull dog days of the Birmingham summer. In the King William Street lectures Newman had been restrained, naturally wanting to play on his audience, not to cause offence. In the Corn Exchange lectures he let his wit, his irony, his way with words run riot, as he lambasted the typical English prejudices, only too recently displayed against Papists and all their works. Roars of laughter could be heard, it was reported, in the streets outside the Corn Exchange, coming from within. The titles of the lectures may sound a bit dull,[6] but do not be put off, the

---

6 e.g. Lecture IV *Fable the Basis of the Protestant View*, or Lecture VIII *Ignorance Concerning Catholics the Protection of the Protestant View*.

text is anything but. Read it now and it is surprising how much, a century and a half later, still reflects the average Englishman's and English woman's, and English journalist's too, instinctive and mainly irrational prejudices—the "old ding-dong" as Newman called it.

These three great trials—the difficulties with establishing the Oratory for the new converts, the Gorham Judgement for the Anglicans, the Papal Aggression for the Catholics—were now, in 1851, to be followed by, from Newman's personal point of view, a greater trial still.

And it was, literally, a trial. Father Newman, Superior of the Birmingham Oratory, famous convert, famous lecturer, was hauled up before the judges of the Queen's Bench in London and given a jail sentence. And it all came about—let lecturers be warned—because of that Lecture V delivered at the Birmingham Corn Exchange on 28 July, a lecture harmlessly enough entitled *Logical Inconsistency of the Protestant View*, rather a dry academic-sounding title.

But Newman spiced it up with a splendid, detailed attack –"Ah! Dr Achilli…"—on that defrocked Dominican friar whose sexual misdeeds Wiseman had already exposed, a year earlier, in the *Dublin Review*. He had taken his precautions. He had asked Hope-Scott, a QC as well as now a convert, if there was any danger of Achilli suing, and Hope-Scott advised him that as it had all been aired before in the *Dublin Review* and as nothing had happened, he could go ahead, lecture and publish without risk.

Never listen to lawyers' advice on libel, however eminent and helpful they may be.[7] Dr Achilli, on 27 October, had Newman served with a High Court writ alleging 23 charges of criminal libel. Newman was prosecuted by the Attorney General and the Solicitor General. Trials, for those who are not lawyers, are no fun at all. Proceedings, particularly in High Court actions, drag on and on. Eighteen months of upset, stress, and fear of jail (Newman was over fifty and physically no hero) followed.

It was in many ways a most extraordinary case. First of all because Achilli was a bad lot, and knew it; and even though backed by the Evangelical Alliance he was almost bound to lose if Newman and his

---

7 Spoken from bitter experience.

friends could gather the evidence. Secondly because it directly involved three future Lord Chief Justices of England—Campbell who tried the case, Cockburn who defended Newman, and Coleridge who passed sentence. And thirdly because against all the evidence[8] Newman, who had pleaded "not guilty" on the grounds of justification, i.e. that what he had alleged was in point of fact true, was found guilty by a jury of good men and true. Even *The Times* this time was appalled by the verdict:

> We consider that a great blow has been given to the administration of justice in this country, and Roman Catholics will have henceforth only too good reason for asserting that there is no justice for them in cases tending to arouse the Protestant feelings of judges and juries.

The trouble was first that Cardinal Wiseman had lost the papers on which he had based his *Dublin Review* article. He was an almost hopelessly disorganised prelate when it came to paperwork, and Newman, most meticulous in this respect, never really forgave him for his assurances, procrastinations, and failures. And secondly that Lord Campbell, "Plain John Campbell", the judge presiding, son of a Calvinist Scots minister from Fife, was unashamedly anti-Catholic and summed up totally against Newman at the end of the five-day trial (which took place in July 1852).

So biased had Campbell been that Newman's defending QC, the small, witty, man-of-the-world Alexander Cockburn, a favourite of Palmerston, much to Campbell's fury applied for a retrial. More delays, suspense, expense, mental anguish. When it came to it, the presiding judge, John Coleridge, a cold, supercilious Eton and Balliol man, refused a new trial and immediately passed sentence, taking the opportunity to give Newman (who at this stage of legal proceedings had no right of reply) a sanctimonious lecture on how his character had morally deteriorated since he had joined the Church of Rome—which must have been peculiarly annoying.[9]

---

8 Witnesses, Italian women and girls who had actually been seduced by Achilli in his days as a Dominican friar, were found (largely by Maria Giberne) and brought to London—at great expense because of the long delays in legal procedure.

9 For all these characters (and indeed many more) see the present author's *Lions under the Throne: The Lord Chief Justices of England.*

So Coleridge J. sentenced Newman to go to jail, or rather to go to jail indefinitely—until he had paid a fine of £100.

Thus in the end Newman was virtually acquitted. His friends and supporters who had crowded the court paid the fine immediately. Newman, much to his relief, walked away a free man.

Newman was invited up to Scotland, to relax after the stresses of the trial. Hope-Scott and his wife invited him to Abbotsford, and Newman spent a warm Christmas sheltering from the frightful weather outside, gales howling, rain splattering, in the low dark rooms and corridors of Sir Walter Scott's baronial fantasy. It was a relaxed time, for there had been great worries about his legal expenses, and though in the end they were to come to £9,000, there were rallies and subscriptions and meetings of support organised not only by Cardinal Wiseman in London and Bishop Ullathorne in Birmingham but all over the world, in Ireland, in France and even in America—and much more than £9,000 eventually came in. It was a sad time, too, though; his sister Harriet had died, never reconciled, and Tom Mozley was now a widower with a little daughter, Grace, Newman's niece, only once seen as a little girl in Oxford.

In the midst of all this, in the summer of 1852, Wiseman had summoned all the new bishops of England together for a Synod, the first coming-together of Catholic bishops in the country since Queen Mary's reign three hundred years earlier.

It was a triumphant moment. Rather wisely, not to appear triumphalist rather than triumphant, the Synod was held not in Westminster but, more discreetly, at Oscott, and the cardinal generously and tactfully invited not one of his bishops to preach, but Newman.

The Second Spring was the title of Newman's famous sermon. The Church dies and the Church blossoms into life again was the general theme. The bishops and clergy were "nearly all in tears"; the cardinal himself "fairly gave up the effort" to control himself "and sobbed like a child."

There were allusions in Newman's sermon, probably conscious, possibly instinctive, to famous sayings or passages. "For where is

Bohun? Where is Mowbray? Where is Mortimer? Nay, which is more and most of all, where is Plantagenet? They are entombed in the arms and sepulchres of mortality" is surely echoed by Newman's "Canterbury has gone its way, and York is gone and Durham is gone and Winchester is gone."

Even more stirringly,

> Then shall our names
> Familiar in his mouth as household words
> Harry the king
> Bedford and Exeter
> Warwick and Talbot
> Salisbury and Gloucester
> Be in their flowing cups freshly remembered.

is recalled in

> Westminster and Nottingham,
> Beverley and Hexham,
> Northampton and Shrewsbury
> If the world lasts,
> Shall be names as musical to the ear
> As stirring to the heart as the glories we have lost
> And Saints shall arise out of them
> If God so will.

And, indeed, it now looks as if a saint shall indeed arise out of them[10] over a century and a half later; and a most unexpected one, not least to the man himself.

---

10 To be pedantic: out of none of the above but out of Birmingham. Less musical to the ear, perhaps?

Intermezzo III

Interlude in Ireland

The "Grecian" Catholic Church he
built in Dublin

"A hornets' nest" John Hungerford Pollen described it as. Or rather: "Newman had a constant sense that he was in a hornets' nest." And who were the hornets? Not the Irish themselves, though many an Englishman in Ireland, particularly at that period, must have felt himself surrounded by hostility and by hatred. Those had been the years of the Great Hunger; over, true, but still a cause of bitter resentment. No, the hornets in question were the Irish bishops, towards whom "Newman on his side preserved an attitude of painstaking politeness".

Irish bishops have never had much of a good press in England. It was true in Restoration England: we executed—hanged, drew and quartered—the Archbishop of Armagh and Primate of All Ireland, Oliver Plunket, at Tyburn on 1 July 1681[1] on entirely trumped-up charges, the fall-out of the (entirely invented) Popish Plot. It is true now. But pity the poor Archbishop of Armagh in 1851, Paul Cullen. It might just as well be said that, by inviting Newman over to Dublin, it was he who introduced a hornet—Newman—into the until then comparatively cosy Irish nest.

And yet it had all begun so well. The background, briefly, was this. The Catholic Irish were woefully undereducated, since Ireland had no university at all, bar Trinity College, Dublin—"a Protestant garrison in a land of Catholics". Peel, as prime minister, had attempted to remedy this by founding three Queen's Colleges, one in Cork, one in Belfast, one in Galway, on totally secular lines. But the Catholic bishops of Ireland were having none of that. Resolutely against Mixed Education—which meant not what we would imagine it now to imply, an old-fashioned term for co-education, but an educational

---

1 St Oliver Plunket's remains are buried in the transept at the Benedictine monastery of Downside Abbey in Somerset—more spectacularly, it must be said, than Bishop Baines'.

system where Catholics and Protestants studied together—they forbade their young men to go to the three Queen's Colleges; and their young men were forbidden—by the other side, so to speak—to enrol at Trinity College, Dublin.

It was an impasse. But in Belgium, newly independent and facing something of the same problem, a group of private citizens had set up, in 1834, a Catholic University at Louvain. It had been a great success. Why, Archbishop Cullen thought, should not a Catholic University be set up in Ireland, in Dublin, on the same lines? And who, under his own overall control of course, should run it? Well, there was one famous university man, a somewhat underemployed university man, now a fellow Catholic priest, in what was now—had been since 1800—the United Kingdom of Great Britain and Ireland. Cullen had been rector of the Irish College in Rome and had come across Newman there. Where would be the harm in trying the idea out on him?

Thus, on 15 April 1851, Cullen wrote to Newman, the great lecturer, to invite him over to Dublin to give a series of lectures against the idea of Mixed Education. On 8 July, Cullen went over to Birmingham, visited the Oratory, brought up the idea of a Catholic University and suggested that Newman should become its rector, in effect—under his supervision as chancellor—its founder. On 12 November, a formal resolution was passed by the assembled Irish bishops endorsing this plan, apparently with enthusiasm.

Understandably, Newman was thrilled. It is not every day that one is asked to found a new university; and for a man whose heart and mind were linked to Oxford, what a chance! Why, he thought, this great new Catholic University of Ireland could become the Catholic university not just for Ireland but for the English-speaking world: not just for Catholics in England and Scotland too, but for those in the colonies—Australia—and indeed ex-colonies—the United States. It was a grandiose vision.

First things, however, first. Peel had imposed his three Queen's Colleges from the top down. Newman knew, from the history of both Oxford and Cambridge, that the best universities grew from small beginnings and from the bottom up—organically, by osmosis, with, of course, an initial push.

In May 1852 he went over to Dublin and there, in the Rotunda, following his usual habit, on a Monday he delivered the first of five lectures, timed as usual at intervals of one a week. He was very nervous about it. But the first, on Monday 10 May, was a great success. "A hit," he described it as, in a letter back to the Birmingham Oratory. "I was heard most distinctly—my voice filled the room. It was just the room I have ever coveted and never had." Or, as Charles Duffy, an Irish listener, put it: "He spoke in a level voice, scarcely raised or lowered by a note, without the play of feature which we regarded as so large a part of Oratory. His speech was a silvery stream which never sank out of view or formed into cascades."

The five Discourses were published fortnightly as separate pamphlets. The Achilli trial intervened. Five more were written but never delivered; again published as pamphlets. All ten Discourses were, that autumn, bound together as one volume and published in February 1853 by John Duffy of Dublin under the title *Discourses on the Scope and Nature of University Education: Addressed to the Catholics of Dublin*.

The ten Discourses are the basis of what, apart from the *Apologia*, is Newman's most famous, most influential and most readable book: *The Idea of a University*. Almost all modern editions[2] are based on the 3rd, London, edition of 1873, where the 5th Discourse was omitted, leaving nine Discourses to form the first part of the book, and ten further occasional lectures and essays[3] to form the second.

There is so much to say about this book that I intend to say almost nothing but simply to quote from Discourse IX, the penultimate section, part of the long tribute that Newman paid to "my own special Father and Patron, St Philip Neri", who, "In the words of his biographer, 'was all things to all men. He suited himself to noble and ignoble, young and old, subjects and prelates, learned and ignorant. When he was called upon to be merry he was so, so that his room went by the agreeable nickname of the Home of Christian Mirth. Nay, people came to him, not only from all parts of Italy, but from

---

2 There are scores of translations too, countless copies particularly, I am told, in American universities where every (?) university has a Newman Room.
3 Originally published separately in 1858 as *Lectures and Essays on University Subjects*. Newman was always tweaking and rearranging his own books.

France, Spain, Germany and all Christendom,; and even the infidels and Jews, who had ever any communication with him, revered him as a holy man.'"

All his life Newman was to pay tribute to St Philip Neri, call upon him to bless the Oratories and the Oratorians and settle their various disputes, celebrate his feast, set him up as an example, invoke him on his death bed. His devotion to St Philip was clearly deep, continuous and heartfelt. This is an aspect of Newman's life and thought that is worth pointing out, for Filippo Neri was no intellectual. Newman, unarguably an intellectual, was no intellectual snob.

That June of 1852 Newman was back in Dublin to attend the celebration and great dinner that marked the installation of Cullen as Archbishop of Dublin. In July he was back again for a fortnight. All seemed set fair.

But then there were inexplicable delays. Weeks, months passed. Nothing happened. Plaintive letters issued from Birmingham; Cullen never answered them. In October 1853 some news eventually came through: the University Committee had raised £2000. But it was not until January 1854 that Archbishop Cullen finally wrote, and after a year and a half's delay the great scheme began at long last to get off the ground.

Why the delay? It was partly Newman's fault. He was, after all, a convert and an Englishman; he felt it was not his place to push. And he never really bothered to study the Irish situation in advance, as no doubt he would have done had he been invited to perform the same role in, say, Spain. In time he came to know the emotions caused by Young Ireland, to learn that Archbishop Cullen's uncle had been hanged in 1798, to realise, if never to appreciate, the power struggle for eventual control of the projected university between the Archbishop of Dublin, very much a Roman by training and inclination, and the Archbishop of Tuam, MacHale, "the Lion of the West". The Irish bishops were divided; there was not sweet unanimity; there were second thoughts.

It was Wiseman, in Rome, who pushed the whole thing forward. He went to see Pio Nono, obtained from him a Pontifical Brief setting up, officially, the Catholic University and appointing Newman as its rector. And furthermore, Wiseman triumphantly wrote, the pope had agreed—in order to give Newman equal standing[4]—to appoint him a bishop: not an administrative bishop with a diocese to run, but the rank of a bishop with a purely nominal see. "*E manderemo a Newman la crocetta*," declared Pio amicably, "*lo faremo vescovo di Porfirio o qualche luogo.*"

The Oratory was thrilled. News leaked. Congratulations poured in. Gifts arrived—from the Duke of Norfolk a massive gold chain. Then no more, ever, was heard. Wiseman never mentioned the matter again. Years later when Maria Giberne, about to become a nun in France, went to Rome for the Holy Father's blessing and boldly—she spoke Italian—tackled him on the subject of Newman's bishopric, Pio Nono looked embarrassed, muttered and turned away. What apparently had happened, as became clear only when history had opened its files, was that the Irish bishops *en masse* had objected to an English cardinal presuming to demand a bishopric for a fellow Englishman that would, in effect, be exercised in Ireland. One can understand their point of view—and Wiseman's impulsiveness, and the pope's embarrassment. Neither Wiseman nor Newman made enough allowance for what Pio Nono was to refer to as the *antipatia raciale* between the English and the Irish.

Bishop or no bishop, the rector designate at last returned to Dublin on 7 February 1854, and though he was continually to be crossing to and fro, there in Dublin he was basically to stay for the next three and a half years.

He was not formally installed as rector until June. Before that, in March, he was back in London to open the Brompton Oratory;[5] and before that, in February, in the worst winter that Ireland had known since 1814, he set out on a tour to meet the Irish bishops.

---

4 What Newman was to call "a blunderbuss in my arsenal".

5 Which immediately, though it was in a village outside London, became extremely successful. The famous church, to Pugin's disgust, was built by Father Faber in the classical style; and to this day the Brompton Oratory has not only survived but flourishes.

It was a trying experience. Newman hated feather beds and mutton, to both of which he was almost invariably treated. Even before he set out there had been a disheartening meeting with the Jesuit Provincial in Dublin; who told him:

> that (1) the class of youths did not exist in Ireland who would come to the University; that the middle class was too poor; that the gentleman class wished a degree for their sons, and sent them to Trinity College;[6] and the upper classes, who were few, sent their sons to English universities etc; that many went abroad, i.e. to Belgium.

"My advice to you," ended the Jesuit, "is this: go to the Archbishop and say: Don't attempt the University—give up the idea."

Generally speaking, the bishops—in Kilkenny, in Carlow, in Waterford, in Cork, in Thurles and in Limerick—were equally discouraging. Newman, cold, tired and dismayed, gave up his planned further trip to confront the "Lion" in Galway.

But he did not give up entirely. He immediately appointed a couple of lecturers, he opened the School of Philosophy and Letters with an initial 17 undergraduates (soon up to 33); he leased Mrs Segrave's house at 6 Harcourt Street and turned it into a small hall of residence with eight undergraduates directly under his own supervision—two French, two Spanish, two English and only two Irish (it seemed the Jesuit had a point); and set up the university itself, the lecture rooms and class rooms, at 86 St Stephen's Green, the tallest house on the most fashionable green in Dublin bought by the Catholic University Committee with money raised from all over Ireland.

6 Harcourt Street, an extension of the green, was rechristened University House, or St Mary's—a bow to the rector's Oxford days. 86 St Stephen's Green because St Patrick's, and 12 Harcourt Street—

---

6 Since Newman had left Oxford, the requirement to subscribe to the 39 Articles had been dropped. Though the hierarchy condemned "Mixed Education", Catholic gentlemen began, bishops or no bishops, to send their sons up to these universities for obvious reasons. As for the degree, one of the eventual reasons for the (comparative) failure of the Catholic University was that it never applied to the government for a charter, and hence any degrees it might give were not officially recognised. Another is that the English Catholics, bar his own personal friends, gave Newman little or none of the support he had counted on.

Father Quinn's Academy, pupils from which were admitted free to the nascent university—became St Laurence's.

The *Catholic University Gazette* came into existence. But necessary though this was, for Newman a University Church was even more essential. He toyed with the idea of a chapel attached to his own University House, but rejected it when he met John Hungerford Pollen, whom he immediately appointed both Professor of Fine Arts and church architect. The garden of 85 St Stephen's Green became available (its owner, a Catholic judge, still an unusual species, Judge Ball, continued to live in No 85 for his lifetime, after which the house too passed to the university) and by amalgamating the gardens of No 85 and No 86 the site for the projected University Church was formed.

"I cannot deny," wrote Newman, "that however my reason may go with Gothic, my heart has ever gone with Grecian. There is in the Italian style such a simplicity, purity, elegance, beauty, brightness that it seems to befit the notion of an angel or a saint;" and, thus, "Is it wonderful that I prefer St Philip to Mr Pugin?"

Pollen, an Englishman, a craftsman, a Fellow of Merton, quite agreed. He became a great friend. What began in Newman's mind as a decorated barn became a basilica that "might almost vie with St Mark's in Venice," thought the overjoyed—perhaps too overjoyed—rector when it finally opened, amazingly quickly, on 1 May 1856. And to Pollen he wrote, "to my taste it is the most beautiful church in the Three Kingdoms." It certainly inspired the choice of style for the Byzantine basilica that is Westminster Cathedral (not, incidentally, to be begun till after Newman's death). It is perhaps Newman's greatest achievement in Dublin and is still the Church of University College, Dublin—though University College, Dublin is very far indeed from the Catholic University of Newman's desire and dreams.

What also survives, and was from the very beginning a great success, is the Cecilia Street Medical School, purchased in the summer of 1856. As Newman put it at the time, of 111 medical practitioners in Dublin only a dozen were Catholics. Dublin, of course, inside the Pale, was still very much a Protestant city. The group of Catholic doctors who purchased Cecilia Street could only do so by using a front-man. Had it been known that Catholics were behind the purchase, it would not have been sold to them. Its great advantage was that it came ready-equipped with operating theatres, dissecting rooms and all the rest of it.

There is a myth, almost unfounded, that Newman wanted to recreate a miniature Oxford in Dublin. Certainly he wished the Catholic University to produce "gentlemen". But gentlemen were to be the end product of a liberal education: what came out, not what went in. Remember the gentlemen-commoners at Oriel for whom Newman had felt only distaste. And his broadness of vision can be seen in the list of the initial 23 professors he appointed. No fewer than eight were medical: Surgery, Anatomy and so forth. There was a chair of Engineering, another of Mathematics, another of Logic. But perhaps Newman's most imaginative appointment was that of the great but ignored Celtic scholar Eugene O'Curry, as Professor of Irish History and Archaeology. Newman would always attend his lectures and encourage him.

There was a Frenchman for French Literature, an Italian for Italian Literature, only two priests (for Theology and Scripture), too many Englishmen as well for the archbishop's taste, and perhaps above all too many supporters of Young Ireland, whom Cullen bracketed with Young Italy, the bane of the Temporal Power and the Papal States.

What really went wrong and what led to Newman's resignation as rector in November 1857[7] was exemplified by these difficulties over the appointment of professors. They were symbolic of that total divergence of views. Here is how a fellow Irishman, Duffy, was to describe the archbishop:

> He had an awkward unimpressive figure and his speech was colloquial and commonplace; but under an unpromising exterior lay a decisive will and overwhelming sense of authority which gave his bearing an air of individuality and power. His idea of government was said to be simple to nudity. Ireland should be ruled, as Rome was ruled, by ecclesiastics, laymen having no function but to contribute a sympathetic ear and deferential audience.

---

7 Despite his urgent wish to quit he postponed his final resignation for a year, on condition that he could live mainly at the Oratory—which needed him back. This absentee rector period worked well neither for him nor for the university nor for the archbishop.

Cullen's ideal university was a lay seminary under his own tight control. Newman's was almost totally the opposite. "If a University is a direct preparation for the world," he had laid it down in one of his Discourses, "let it be what it professes. It is not a Convent, not a Seminary, it is a place to fit men of the world for the world."

It was inevitable that the two men should clash and that the man who had the power should exercise it. In the autumn of 1857 Newman left Ireland. Technically the Catholic University had failed. In the rector's last year there were still only 100 undergraduates or so (though there were not many more in the Queen's Colleges in Cork and Galway either). But I think Newman had, perhaps too late, come to have a feeling for Ireland. In his last lecture to his evening class students, he spoke of Ireland's "people of great natural abilities, keen-sighted, original and subtle" and perorated with evident sincerity on "the wrongs of the oppressed".

Many years later, after 1883 when the Jesuits had taken over the Catholic University,[8] Newman wrote back to that greatest of all English Jesuits, Gerard Manley Hopkins, who was lecturing there—and uneasy—at the time. "There is one consideration you omit," he responded. "The Irish patriots hold that they have never yielded themselves to the sway of England and therefore never have been under her laws, and never have been rebels. If I were an Irishman, I should be at heart a rebel."

For the Englishman through and through whose greatest bugbear had once been Daniel O'Connell the Liberator, it was quite an admission.

---

8 Which they were to run until 1909.

Chapter Five

From Dark Days to
Fame Unforeseen

Manning: from archdeacon to second
Archbishop of Westminster

1860 was a black year for the Catholic aristocracy.

First the 14th Duke of Norfolk died—"the most pious layman of our time" —and he was only 45. Not that he had always been pious, but a trip to Paris as a young man had, rather paradoxically, brought him back to his Catholic ways; and in the great controversy over the Papal Aggression ten years earlier he had, as an MP, voted against his party, his prime minister Lord John Russell and his father in the Lords. His Protestant wife, Minna, had also converted, thanks to Father Faber at the London Oratory. She presented him with a set of gold vestments as a sign of gratitude. "People are beginning to call and notice us because of Lady Arundel's[1] conversion," wrote Faber to Newman, "how small!"

The Arundels had been fellow-guests of Newman that Christmas at Abbotsford when he was relaxing away from the strains of the Achilli trial, and Minna had obviously been impressed. When her husband died—he had only been duke for four years, and very ill for two of these, with Father Faber continually rushing down to Arundel Castle to comfort him—she decided to send her son to the Oratory School that Newman had opened the year before, cheek by jowl to the Oratory in Birmingham.

At the age of thirteen the boy became the 15th Duke of Norfolk, and the leading ornament, at least socially speaking, of the new school. He was rather quiet and shy. He had three boisterous sisters; and to become Premier Duke of England, with a string of titles, a pile of castles and a swathe of estates, as well as the leading Catholic layman in the land, must have been rather overwhelming.

---

1   The eldest son of the Duke of Norfolk takes the "courtesy title" of Earl of Arundel, but remains legally a commoner not a peer; and therefore is entitled (if elected) to sit in the House of Commons.

The Oratory School had become Newman's pet project since his return from Ireland. The fees were eighty guineas a year, not a great strain on the Norfolk finances then. It was to be run on the lines of Eton, with Tutors and Dames, and it was to become successful enough, though never a Catholic Eton. But it was also to give Newman continual headaches and heartaches for years to come. At one stage he had to become headmaster himself, until Ambrose St John relieved him. The administrative problems, the correspondence, the difficulties with staff—l'Abbé Rougemont, the French master, turned out, after he had flitted with the boys' savings, not to have been a priest at all—took up an enormous amount of Newman's time and energy. Much of which went too—the time especially, many hours a week—on hearing confessions from the normal parishioners and the other usual round of parish duties.

The young duke at least was, in later years, to show his gratitude. But what, one wonders, ever became of the gold chain his father had presented to Newman when the rumour was out of Newman being about to become a bishop? History, unless in unsorted Arundel Castle archives, does not relate.

The second death in 1860 was that of Maria, widow of Sir Richard Acton, 7th baronet. Maria was no ordinary English country squire's wife, and of course the Actons were no ordinary Shropshire squires. Maria was the only child and heiress of the Duke of Dahlberg. Or, to give him his full and glorious title, Emerich Josef Franz Heinrich Dismus Kammerich Baron and Duke of Dahlberg, nephew also of the Elector of Mainz, Primate of the Confederation of the Rhine.

On his mother's death Sir John Acton, aged sixteen, was hence not only possessor of Aldenham and the Shropshire estates and the Palazzo Acton in Naples which he had inherited from his father as a child of three, but now also of the *Schloss* at Herrnsheim on the Rhine, of vast possessions in the Rhineland and, in France, of the Hôtel Dahlberg on the Faubourg St Honoré. In other words a young man in possession of great wealth, with houses and relatives all over Europe, with an uncle a cardinal, a grandfather famous throughout southern Italy, and a stepfather—Earl Granville, his mother's second husband—a great Whig peer and man of the world. He was the sort of young man in fact who might almost be destined to follow the father he had barely known, and his fashionable mother, into the world of high society, gambling, racing—or perhaps even politics. Acton, even more than the young Duke of Norfolk, had the world, or at least Europe, at his feet.

But Acton was half-German by blood and an extremely serious young man. At the age of fourteen he went to study under and lodge with Dr Döllinger in Munich. Of Döllinger the boy wrote to his mother: "He is unquestionably the most cool-headed man I ever knew. His judgement is singularly original and independent. He prefers Byron to Milton, and thinks Wellington the greatest of modern generals. He is minutely conversant with English literature." It is a letter that says more about the mind of the fourteen-year-old, it seems to me, than it does about that of his professor. In Munich Dr Döllinger, and therefore indirectly young Acton, was visited by James Hope-Scott, and also by John Hungerford Pollen. The first meeting with Newman himself appears not to have been until the summer of 1858, two years after Acton had been, with his stepfather, on a highly social, highly successful trip to Moscow as part of the official British delegation to the coronation of Tsar Alexander II.

Dr Döllinger was staying with Acton at Aldenham, and they both visited the oratory at Birmingham. Newman was twice Acton's age and more, but there was no question of this particularly highly self-possessed young man becoming in any sense Newman's disciple. Instead, Acton involved him in a venture that was to cause Newman only grief.

Newman was at something of a loose end in that summer of 1858. Though still officially rector, he had in fact left Ireland. The Oratory School was not to occupy his mind until the following year; intellectually he was without stimulus. Acton was thinking of taking over the *Dublin Review* but Newman dissuaded him: "a dreary publication," he wrote, "which wakes up to growl or lecture and then goes to sleep again." But Newman did show "intense interest" in *The Rambler*, another minor Catholic publication, when Acton set about taking that over.

Newman had edited *The British Critic* for almost four years and, more recently, the *Catholic University Gazette*, rather a successful publication too. No wonder he found *The Rambler* project attractive. But *The Rambler* was a liberal magazine run by laymen; Newman was a priest, under obedience. Acton was self-assured enough and wealthy enough to brush aside or to ignore criticism from the clergy. Newman, with the apparent failure of the Catholic University project, had lost much of his self-confidence. From February 1858 until June 1859 Newman was involved with *The Rambler* and with Acton, and, with defending articles in *The Rambler* that gave great offence to Cardinal Wiseman, to the bishops in general and even to Newman's own bishop, usually his firm supporter, the canny Bishop Ullathorne. It all came to a head with the editor being forced to resign, threatened with a spate of Pastorals from the pulpits, the March 1859 issue being suppressed, and Newman himself taking over, somewhat reluctantly, as editor for the two following months. The May issue went well, but the June issue did not. His article *On Consulting the Faithful in Matters of Doctrine* was denounced to Propaganda by a Bishop Brown as heretical. Wiseman, in Rome, promised to sort it out but, as usual, forgot. And Newman, originally greeted in Rome as a new ornament of the Church, now became darkly suspect, under a cloud.

As for *The Rambler*, Acton closed it down in April 1862 and founded a political and literary Catholic monthly, the *Home and Foreign Review*, to replace it. Acton was now in the House of Commons, Whig member for Carlow in Ireland, disapproving of his own leader, the racy Palmerston—even more so of the rising Tory star Disraeli (who had satirised Ambrose Phillipps in his novel *Coningsby* as the limp Sir Eustace Lyle of Saint Genevieve Manor), and about to initiate that close friendship with Mr Gladstone that was to remain for the rest of their mutual lives.

"I beg of you," wrote Acton from the House of Commons to Newman at one moment of crisis, "remembering the difficulties you encountered, to consider my position in the midst of a hostile and illiterate episcopacy, an ignorant clergy, a prejudiced and divided laity, with the cliques at Brompton, York Place, Ushaw always on the watch."

They were on the watch now for Newman too.

Back in 1851, in his first flush of delight with the whole Irish scheme, Newman had offered that new convert Manning the post of vice-rector—in effect his second-in-command at the Catholic University. "My dear Newman," Manning had replied, politely refusing, "Your note has set me wishing to do anything you bid me. I need to say that old affections and many debts draw me strongly towards you." But "On 3rd November I trust to start for Rome. Do not forget me."

Wiseman had been overjoyed at the archdeacon's conversion, and less than ten weeks later, without the usual months of preparation, personally ordained the new convert a priest. To and fro to Rome Manning did indeed travel, continuously. He was a man who had great charm, great abilities. Pio Nono, most impressed, wanted to hold onto him in Rome as a Papal Chamberlain. But Manning was already beginning to make himself indispensable to Cardinal Wiseman, who was hopeless as an administrator. It was Dr Whitty, the Irishman Newman had so liked, the priest who in Wiseman's absence had taken the decision to circulate the Pastoral *From Out the Flaminian Gate*—"I was young and inexperienced," pleaded Whitty, humbly, after the damage had been done—who proposed that Manning should replace him as Vicar General. Manning thus became not Newman's right hand man in Dublin, but the cardinal's right hand man at York Place, Wiseman's London residence. It was a far better, far wiser choice.

At the same time—1857—Manning, taking an obvious leaf out of Newman's book, founded a Congregation in Bayswater and was elected its superior. He had been to Milan, studied what Carlo Borromeo had done, and came back to found the Oblates of St Charles. "They will in fact be the Jesuits of London," explained Manning, hubristically, to Hope-Scott, "and I propose they should be simple priests." Soon enough there were twenty of them, four new churches in and around Bayswater, and 346 converts—the new Vicar General kept a locked notebook with all the names carefully listed, including the Duchess of Buccleuch and the Duchess of Argyll. Manning was rechristened in polite society "The Apostle to the Genteels".

But Manning too had his fall. He was too much of a disciplinarian, he had risen too fast, and when his oblates took over St Edmund's Ware with the cardinal's blessing (and thus the education of all would-be priests in what had been the London District) a furious reaction against his, and their, "tyranny" set in.

Bishop Errington, an Old Catholic and a Canon Lawyer, had been at school with Wiseman. Generous, impulsive Wiseman had appointed him his coadjutor bishop, with right of succession. In other words Errington was going to be, come what may, the next Archbishop of Westminster. He and the canons of the Westminster Archdiocese naturally enough objected to Manning, and Manning alone, having the cardinal's ear.

The vicissitudes that followed ruined the now-ailing cardinal's last years. The disputes went to Rome. The oblates had to be pulled out of St Edmund's Ware. But Errington, a fine man who would, it seems, have made an excellent archbishop, offended the pope unforgivably by, only too lawyer-like, taking out a notebook and recording notes of the private conversation he and the pontiff were having while they were having it.

The end result was that Errington was stripped of the right of succession. As consolation prize he was offered the Archbishopric of Trinidad, which he turned down. Obedient to authority he resigned and was eventually to become a humble priest in the Isle of Man. The poor old cardinal heaved a great sigh of relief and retired more and more to his country retreat, leaving his Vicar General to manage the archdiocesan affairs.

As Manning's star rose, dipped and rose again, Newman's dismally faded and waned. He had written another novel, *Callista - A Tale of the Third Century,* begun before Dublin, finished and published during. Set in Newman's favourite century and part of the world— North Africa—it was the story of a martyrdom. Triumphant in the heroine Callista's case—but not triumphant at all in what he rather felt was becoming his own. For the cardinal had proposed he should undertake a translation of the Bible. Newman had set about it and then, once again, nothing more had been heard. So he was writing nothing—except, of course, letters. He was doing in a small way much but achieving in a large way little. He seems to have forgotten, at least partly, St Philip's injunction always to be cheerful. He was passing through what in another man might have been his own dark night of the soul.

To Isabel Froude, Hurrell's niece and, with her husband, a convert, he wrote at about this time:

> I have not the faith, patience and resignation that I ought to have. It is so bad to be simply passive in suffering.
>
> Thirty years have passed since I have been a sort of target for a shot when any one wished to try his hand, and had nothing better to do. I used as a Protestant to say that no-one except O'Connell was so well-abused as I. I have tried to do works for God year after year and for thirty years they have all failed. Now the evening has come, and I have done nothing. It is most difficult to go on working in the face of thirty years' disappointment. Everything seems to crumble under my hands, as if one were making ropes of sand.

Emily Bowles, a little later, was writing to Newman about Acton: "He does so lament—he does so fully appreciate—what we all lose in your silence." She added on her own behalf the *cri de coeur*. "Why should you be out there—so far away from us all?"

To which Newman replied with a long, long scroll equally heartfelt but much more analytical and detailed than in his reply to Isabel Froude. Yes, he had lost all his influence but, had he been in the conflict, "I should come into collision with everyone I met. I should be treading on everyone's toes." As for Propaganda, "too rough and ready, it likes quick results—scalps from beaten foes by the hundred." "Sometimes," he ended, surprised at how he had been going on,[2] "I seem to myself inconsistent in professing to love retirement, yet

---

2 "I never wrote such a letter to anyone yet"—quite an admission for such a letter writer—"and I shall think twice before I send you the whole of it." But send it he did. Frederick Bowles, one of his original band and Emily's brother, had left the Oratory a year or two earlier, in 1860, which had added much to Newman's dismay.

seemingly impatient at doing so little. Then I say 'Perhaps I am hiding my talent in a napkin'. Next people say to me 'Why are you not doing more? How much you could do!' and then, since I think I could do a great deal if I was let to do it, I become uneasy. And lastly, willing as I am to observe St Philip's dear rule that 'we should despise being despised', yet when I find that scorn and contempt become the means of *my Oratory being injured*, I get impatient."

Those are not the words of a soul desolate, in the valley of the shadow. They were certainly dark days for Newman, but a dark night of the soul? Not in the traditional sense.

Moreover, things were about to change. Indeed now after six years of somnolence the Leopard of Birmingham was about to spring into fierce action once again.

It was a packet that arrived in the post on the cold morning of 30 December 1863 that first pricked him out of his lethargy. Inside the packet was an advance copy of the January issue of *Macmillan's Magazine*. Inside the magazine was a long and enthusiastic review of J.A. Froude's—Hurrell's youngest brother—*History of England from the time of Henry VIII to the Spanish Armada*. And inside the review there was this passage, marked in pencil:

> Truth, for its own sake, has never been a virtue with the Roman clergy. Father Newman informs us that it need not, and on the whole ought not to be. Whether his notion be doctrinally correct or not, it is at least historically so.

The packet was sent anonymously;[3] and the review was signed only with the initials C.K. Newman said to himself: "Here is a young scribe who is making himself a cheap reputation by smart hits at safe objects." He stretched out a mildly indignant paw, and sent a letter of protest at such a "grave and gratuitous slander" to Messrs Macmillan.

---

3   In fact by a Catholic priest in Yorkshire, Father Pope, like Newman both a convert and a former Anglican clergyman.

But in fact C.K. was not a young scribe, and C.K. already had a great reputation; C.K. was Professor of Modern History at Cambridge; C.K. was the author of *Hypatia,* a novel much on the lines of, and much more successful than, Newman's *Callista.* C.K. was also the author of two of the most popular novels of the time, *Westward Ho* and *The Water Babies*; C.K. was an Anglican clergyman, Rector of Eversley in Hampshire; C.K. was the famous Charles Kingsley.

"Reverend Sir," wrote Newman on 7 January, "when I received your letter, taking upon yourself the authorship, I was amazed. I am, Reverend Sir, Your obedient servant, John H Newman."

The row escalated. The Reverend Sirs exchanged outwardly polite but barbed letters. Kingsley harked back to a sermon Newman had preached over twenty years before and was prepared to issue a semi-apology, with which, he wrote, "I have done as much as one English gentleman can expect from another." Newman was beginning to enjoy himself and sketched an invented dialogue.

Mr Kingsley relaxes: "Do you know, I like your *tone*. From your *tone* I rejoice, greatly rejoice, to believe that you did not mean what you said."

I rejoin: "*Mean* it! I maintain I never said it, whether as a Protestant or a Catholic."

Mr Kingsley replies: "I waive that point."

I object: "Is it possible? What? Waive the main question? I either said it or I didn't. You have made a monstrous charge against me direct, distinct, public.

You are bound to prove it as directly, as distinctly, as publicly; or to own you can't."

Newman, with Kingsley's permission, published the correspondence. Kingsley, rather rashly, launched a counter-attack—a pamphlet of 33 pages entitled *What, Then, Does Dr Newman Mean?*, an angry little production. It came out on 20 March. On 16 April Newman set out to write a rebuttal, a "History of My Opinions". He had, in the intervening weeks, written to his old friends from Tractarian days asking for copies of his letters and theirs, assembling his materials.

He wrote, when he began writing, at fever pitch, almost non-stop, standing at his desk in his room at the Birmingham Oratory. And every Thursday, from 21 April to 2 June, Messrs Longman published as a pamphlet what he had written earlier that week.

The first of these pamphlets was entitled *Mr Kingsley's Method of Disputation*, the next *True Mode of Meeting Mr Kingsley*, and the last, published as an Appendix and detailing 39 "Blots" or factual errors, *Answer in Detail to Mr Kingsley's Accusations*. But the heart of what was to become, shortened, omitting the pamphlets listed above, omitting even Kingsley's name, the *Apologia pro Vita Sua* were the sections headed *History of My Religious Opinions*: up to 1833; from 1833 to 1839; from 1839 to 1841; from 1841 to 1845—after which: "From the time that I became a Catholic, of course I have no further history of my religious opinions to narrate."

Summarised in this way, the *Apologia* may sound dry as dust. It is not. It is sparkling, witty, moving, intensely personal. It is written very much in the conversational style of the dialogue quoted above. At the end of the first pamphlet comes the magnificent, killer sweep of the claw that demolished, almost at a stroke, the wretched author of *The Water Babies*. "And now I am in a train of thought higher and more serene than any which slanders can disturb. Away with you, Mr Kingsley, and fly into space. Your name shall occur again as little as I can help, in the course of these pages."

And in the next, a magnificent, roaring, appeal:

Mankind has the right to judge of Truthfulness in the case of a Catholic as in the case of a Protestant, of an Italian, or of a Chinese. I think, indeed, Englishmen the most suspicious and touchy of mankind; I think them unreasonable and unjust in their seasons of excitement.

But I had rather be an Englishman (as in fact I am) than belong to any other race under heaven.

They are as generous as they are hasty and burly; and their repentance of their injustice is greater than their sin.

The Reverend Kingsley did not repent; at least not publicly. But he knew when he was beat; he was conscious that, like the impulsive Rupert of Hentzau, facing, pistol in hand, back to the wall, the righteously self-confident and utterly merciless Rudolf Rassendyll, he had met his match in Newman. He had been totally outclassed and reduced, almost, to a pitiful figure of derision.

As for Newman, at a bound he had emerged from the shadows. It took him some time to realise the vastness of his triumph. Anglicans and Catholics alike, old friends and total unknowns, wrote in their hundreds to congratulate him, to say that they both, now, by reading the *Apologia*, understood each other's positions and emotions much more clearly. In America fans even began christening their babies Newman. From this time onwards Newman was a star not only in but of the Catholic world—perhaps (to end the metaphor) the only holy leopard who has ever so successfully and so publicly changed his religious spots.

While the stream of pamphlets that were to form the *Apologia* were coming out and causing such a stir in the literary and clerical world, there were storms thundering over the wider political and religious heavens.

Garibaldi came to London to a hero's welcome. Cardinal Wiseman issued a Pastoral both against his visit and against, even more—there was no episcopal ecumenical soft-soapery in those robust days—the welcome extended to Garibaldi by the bishops of the Church of England.

Why? I have tried to avoid in this short book too much use of technical terms. But in this case the outburst was all to do with the Temporal Power. Which was, briefly, this: the pope was ruler not just of the Vatican as now but of all Rome—and also of the Papal States. Thus, for example, Pio Nono's successor-to-be, Leo XIII, had been, as bishop, papal governor first of Benevento to the south of Rome, and then of Perugia to the north. The theory was that the Papal States were vital to the independence of the pope. Without them, without the Temporal Power, without his position as an independent monarch in a Europe of monarchies, he would be a puppet of one or other of the Catholic powers of the day, of the Bourbons of Spain, the Hapsburgs of Austria or even of Louis Napoleon of France.

But the Temporal Power was under threat. It is perhaps hard to picture nowadays a Europe where neither Italy nor Germany existed as nation-states but only as a conglomeration of minor kingdoms, dukedoms, principalities and republics. The move towards unity was, however, on—and, arguably, it was a fatal move. Had Germany never been united (as it was about to be by Bismarck and Prussia) would the world have been a worse, or a better, place?

Catholics certainly felt that way—worse—about the unifying of Italy by Cavour and Vittorio Emmanuele of Savoy in the north and by Garibaldi in the south, squeezing down on the Papal States, ruining the Temporal Power and aiming at a second, and this time perpetual, "liberation" of Rome—reducing Pio Nono (who had sworn never to quit Rome again) to a frustrated and impotent figurehead.

Mr Gladstone had been instrumental in rousing English public opinion against the horrors of King "Bomba" and his gruesome prisons in the south; and indeed Bomba's son and heir, "Bombino", had swiftly lost the Kingdom of the Two Sicilies to Garibaldi's liberating Red Shirts. Italian Unity was all the cry. But Italian Unity inevitably now involved the ruin of the Temporal Power, and all good Catholics were called upon to oppose it and to support the pope.

Those who supported the pope and the Temporal Power fervently, totally, were known as the Ultramontanes, a term meaning, literally, "beyond the mountains", presumably the far side of those "windswept Apennines"—as if they were themselves, heart and soul and body and mind, ensconced in the Eternal City, protected by the marshes and dusty plains of the Romagna.

The Ultramontanes, of course, supported even more fervently the spiritual powers of the pope.

Opposed to the Ultramontanes were the liberals, often known as the Gallicans, the French party, within the Catholic Church. Acton, despite his family connections with the Bourbons of the Two Sicilies, was a liberal; so was Dr Döllinger. Cardinal Wiseman, a Roman of the Romans by taste and upbringing, was an Ultramontane; so was his Vicar General, Monsignor (as he had now become) Manning.

The battle-lines were being drawn—and not only in the temporal trenches defending the gradually-eroding Papal States.

The Pastoral was to be Cardinal Wiseman's swansong. He was ill, and on 2 February 1865 a telegram reached Manning in Rome to say that the cardinal was dying and that he was the cardinal's literary executor.

On 15 February Wiseman died. His funeral showed that Newman had been so right the year before when he had described the English as being as generous as they were hasty. The man who had been execrated and burnt in effigy fifteen years earlier could have seen his funeral procession watched, even applauded, by thousands of Londoners as it wended its way through the streets from Brompton Oratory (where Manning, back in time, had preached the funeral sermon[4]) to its burial place in Kensal Green. The burning question was, of course, immediately raised: who was to be the next Archbishop of Westminster?

Newman's name was even suggested by some, so famous had he suddenly become. But a convert as the second archbishop? Hardly! And in any case Newman's *forte* was not, never had been, administration. Capable and hard-working though he had proved himself, his heart was never totally in it.

The system for selection of a new archbishop was this: the Chapter of the Westminster archdiocese would have to propose to Rome the trium: three names which they would label, in order of preference, *dignus, dignior, dignissimus*. The final choice then was up to the Vatican, in effect up to the Cardinal Prefect of Propaganda. Provocatively, the canons of the Chapter proposed as *dignissimus* Bishop Errington, the very man the pope had personally deprived of his automatic right of succession. Confusion followed. Bishop Grant, *dignus,* let it be known he would not accept. There were even rumours about Manning. "Manning is no more than an aspiring refugee from a hostile camp," proclaimed *The Tablet,* damningly, whereas "Bishop Clifford will be welcomed by thoroughbred Catholics as a legitimate and hereditary ruler." Clifford was an Old Catholic—a Clifford of Chudleigh, perhaps too hereditary. Bishop Ullathorne was proposed as a compromise candidate and seemed the undoubted favourite.

---

4 Father Faber had died two years before, in 1863. Newman, sceptical—"How many times has Faber been a-dying?"—eventually visited him on his deathbed and the two were reconciled. Faber was only 59 but had become very fat.

But then Pio Nono stepped in directly and took the decision out of everyone else's hands into his own. "The Pope had seldom given a clearer proof of his fallibility," came the commentary upon what was to many the astounding and most unwelcome news.

On 8 June Manning was consecrated second Archbishop of Westminster by Bishop Ullathorne. He had spent the previous week at Highgate in retreat, conducting an intense and extremely critical self-examination, taking as his guide Bishop Challoner's *Memoirs of Missionary Priests*. He had made himself ill. He looked at his consecration almost at death's door himself.

"Manning's rise is marvellous," commented Newman, privately and a little acidly. "In fourteen years a Protestant Archdeacon is made Catholic Archbishop of Westminster." He only barely agreed to attend the consecration, provided he was spared the celebratory lunch afterwards. Archbishop Manning was soon to calm almost all his opponents with his courtesy, new-found consideration and considerable charm.

But not Newman. Never indeed Newman. For the truth was that, in the months before, between the *Apologia's* triumph and the new archbishop's consecration, Manning had blocked, had stymied Newman's dearest dream.

Oxford had always been Newman's earthly City of God; more so than Birmingham, Dublin, or even, I would venture, than Rome. The *Apologia* had been published in the spring of 1864. In August, almost out of the blue, Newman was offered a five-acre site in the centre of Oxford, a vast stretch of real estate between St Giles' and Walton Street. The price was high—over £8000. But Hope-Scott almost at once offered a thousand pounds, and the delighted Bishop Ullathorne, in whose diocese of Birmingham Oxford fell and who had always been ashamed that Oxford had only one poor Catholic Chapel in St Clement's, at once proposed to Newman the Oxford Mission.

"We want to erect a great centre of Catholicism in Oxford," wrote an inspired Newman to another subscriber, "which may last and grow ever more important as time goes on."

But the authorities squashed it. An Oratory Mission in Oxford[5] and an Oratory Church would inevitably mean Newman's return to Oxford. And Newman's return would as inevitably draw in its wake hordes of young Catholic men to be faced with those dangers of a "Mixed Education" so carefully avoided at Dublin.

The examples of two Catholic undergraduates of good family who had gone off the rails at Oxford were cited to Propaganda.[6] Propaganda was used to the secular, ferociously anti-clerical, anti-Catholic universities of Northern Europe and assumed, wrongly but reasonably, that Oxford was much the same. Newman had bought the land in October and written, enormously bucked, to a friend in November that: "There is just now a very remarkable feeling in my favour at Oxford"—even among his ancient foes, the Heads of Houses. Moreover: "An undergraduate writes to me: 'There is a report that you were at Oriel last Friday incognito; it caused great excitement.'" All the worse was the disappointment when Propaganda finally vetoed the scheme. Bitterly, somewhat unjustly, Newman put it down, once again, to the "dull tyranny of Manning and Ward"— that W.G. Ward who had succeeded him as leader of the Oxford Movement, then converted, resigned his fellowship, married, had been found a job at St Edmund's Ware by Wiseman, and was now both an ultra Ultramontane and the highly partisan editor of the *Dublin Review*.

"On the morning of the 23rd," Newman wrote in the *Apologia*, referring back to the year 1843, "I left the Observatory. I have never seen Oxford again, excepting its spires, as they are seen from the railway."

---

5 Failure then, success now. The Oxford Mission was awarded to the Jesuits. The Marquess of Bute, a convert, offered land next to what was until 2009 the Radcliffe Infirmary on Woodstock Road. Bishop Ullathorne laid the foundation stone of St Aloysius' Church (in the style of the Chiesa dell'Jesu in Rome) in 1871. In 1981 the Jesuits handed over the church to the Archbishop of Birmingham. In 1990, the hundredth anniversary of Newman's death, Archbishop Couve de Murville passed it on to the Birmingham Oratory. And now the Oxford Oratory is a flourishing independent oratory of its own—the third in the country— and the closest, one might hazard, to the heart of the blessed John Henry as he looks down from above.
6 Young Charles Weld-Blundell had left Christ Church with—it was reported in Rome— debts of no less than £7000 (hard to believe—an enormous sum) and an actress (less so).

Nor, over twenty years later, was he to do so now. Oriel's undergraduates could not, as planned, welcome him back with a great procession. The only consolation—but an important one—was that the following February the university bought the site for £9000, clearing Newman's debt totally.

Where precisely those five acres were I find it difficult to picture. Behind Blackfriars and Pusey House and the Ashmolean? Or perhaps further up? Including the land—perhaps half an acre, certainly no more—on which the present Oxford Oratory stands?

Chapter Six

From a Dream of Death
to Earthly Eminence

Cardinal Newman, robed and aged

One pleasing side-effect of the *Apologia*, and indeed of the failed Oxford attempt, was renewed friendship with old Tractarian friends. Frederick Rogers and Richard Church, both Anglican vicars, gave Newman the most tactful and welcome of gifts—a violin. Actually they asked him to choose the violin for himself and paid the bill. He called it a fiddle, and he was delighted after so many years to fiddle away again. In later years Dean Church's children (Mr Gladstone was to appoint Church Dean of St Paul's) Helen, Mary and Edith became friends of his old age, sending him *Alice in Wonderland*, a perfect choice for a logician like Newman. For a man for whom friendship was so important and loss of friendship such a blow this was a wonderful change.

But of course he had no idea that he was going to live to such a venerable old age. His thoughts were turning, with the *Apologia* his spiritual autobiography safely behind him, to the Four Last Things. That January, the January of 1865, he began writing "on scraps of paper" what was to become his finest poem, *The Dream of Gerontius*.

Like the *Apologia*, it was an amazing and instant success when first published in May and June in two instalments in the Jesuit literary journal *The Month* and later, on All Souls Day, 2 November, as a whole—a long poem, but not excessively so, of 900 lines, equal approximately to one book of Homer's *Iliad*, Gladstone's favourite reading. "I own," wrote Gladstone to Newman, "that it seems to me the most remarkable production since the unapproachable *Paradiso* of Dante and his less wonderful *Purgatorio*." Even the ranks of Tuscany could scarce forbear to cheer. "I have read *The Dream of Gerontius* with awe and admiration," wrote Kingsley to a friend, "however much I may differ from the *entourage* in which Newman's present creed surrounds the present idea, I must feel that central idea is as true as it is noble."

Newman's prose, an astute critic has pointed out, is in style much more poetic than his poetry, which the critic rightly describes as rhetorical. What makes *The Dream* such an interesting, and easy, read is its unusual plot. It has great similarities to the *Ars Moriendi* of the Middle Ages. An old man, Gerontius, is dying, and as in the *Ars Moriendi* the deathbed is surrounded by Assistants and, at the end, a Priest. Then the Soul, not quite sure whether it is alive or dead, is watched over kindly by Gerontius' Angel, who escorts him up towards the judgement seat, through a hub-hub of Demons (such as those clustered round the deathbed in the *Ars Moriendi*) and up through Choirs of Angelicals—five of them, no less, all singing "Praise to the Holiest in the Height"—via the Angels of the Sacred Stair into the presence of the Angel of the Agony. As in a Greek tragedy, the action—the judgement—takes place off-stage; and the Angel, compassionately, lowers his "dearest sweetest soul" into the waters (not, incidentally, the flames) of Purgatory, with a consolatory

> Be brave and patient on thy bed of sorrow
> And I will come and wake thee on the morrow.

A year later Gerard Manley Hopkins, up at Balliol, wrote to "Very Reverend Father" at Birmingham to enquire about being received—despite the worrying opposition of his parents. He followed up with a visit. "Dr Newman was most kind," he wrote to a friend, "I mean in the very best sense, for his manner is not that of solicitous kindness, but genial and almost, so to speak, unserious." Newman received the young man into the Church a few months later. *The Wreck of the Deutschland*, written ten years later when Hopkins was training to become a Jesuit, was turned down by *The Month* for its weird scansion and general breaking of every received rule. It is unarguably a far greater poem than *The Dream of Gerontius*.

But *The Dream* is so unusual. Who thought then, who thinks now, even among committed Christians, about exactly what happens to us after death? We cannot know, of course, but Newman boldly imagined, and, as the prime minister implied, nobody since Dante had done that in such a symbolically detailed and convincing way.

Those who sing "Praise to the Holiest in the Height" should know that there are thirty verses, and that they are only singing the Fifth Choir of Angelicals. Those who sing "Firmly I Believe and Truly" should know that they are singing what Gerontius declaimed on his deathbed. And those who sing neither but perhaps go to hear Elgar's great choral work should know that it was written between January and June 1900, ten years after Newman had himself faced the Angel of the Agony, and first performed at the Birmingham Triennial Festival. (That first performance, incidentally, was a disaster.)

In 1868 there were great celebrations to mark the coming of age of the Duke of Norfolk. Ambrose St John, as his former headmaster, went up to Norfolk House in London to represent the Fathers of the Oratory. "The Father"—as the superior of the oratory, the provost, is traditionally known by his fellow priests—stayed in Birmingham. He was ageing now, and besides he was engaged in writing the most ambitious and most difficult of all his books, *The Grammar of Assent*.[1] Above all, he was trying to avoid becoming personally embroiled in the horrid controversies that were tearing the whole Catholic world apart.

It was not now merely the question of the Temporal Power of the papacy, bitterly though that was being fought out, both literally on the ground and metaphorically in men's minds. It was also, even more so, the rising melodrama of the spiritual power of the pope. There had already been—on 8 December 1854—the proclamation by Papal Bull and *ex cathedra* of the Immaculate Conception of Our Lady.[2] There had been, ten years later, the Encyclical *Quanta Cura* and the attached *Syllabus of Errors*. And now there was to be a General Council at which the great question of defining and proclaiming the infallibility of the pope would be decided

Infallibility is not impeccability, muttered Newman drily. All Catholics, Newman included, accepted the infallibility of the Teaching

1 Basically a study of the relationship between Faith and Reason. It finally came out in 1870. It had been on Newman's mind for many years as underpinning his whole thought. It is not light reading.
2 Not to be confused, as even many Catholics are liable to confuse it, with the doctrine of the Virgin Birth.

Church in general—*Ecclesia docens*. But was it necessary to provoke, to define, to lay down the infallibility of the pope? And, came the unspoken thought in the minds of the liberals, of such a pope as Pio Nono had become? Was the *Syllabus of Errors* to be retrospectively declared infallible teaching? The Ultramontanes certainly hoped so. Newman, no lover of liberalism and quietly sceptical about the necessity of the Temporal Power, thought in general that "It is not good for a Pope to live twenty years. He becomes a god, has no-one to contradict him, and does cruel things without meaning it."

Furthermore Newman held that an Ecumenical Council should only be called when it was absolutely necessary—to condemn a heresy, as with the early councils, to define a doctrine or dogma challenged, as at Trent; not just, so to speak, at the whim of the Vatican. He was an "inopportunist" and felt that it was not necessary at all to call the First Vatican Council. And undoubtedly he would have felt exactly the same about the Second Vatican Council had he still been alive eighty years later.

Bishops and cardinals converged on Rome. Newman had been invited to attend as a *peritus,* an expert adviser. Wisely he refused. Laymen and liberals converged too—Acton and Dr Döllinger among them. The First Vatican Council opened on the recently proclaimed Feast of the Immaculate Conception, 8 December 1869. Unfortunately for himself Newman was to write in early January a long and private letter to Bishop Ullathorne in Rome.

It did not remain private. Weeks later he was writing to Ambrose Phillipps, a fellow "inopportunist".

I am in somewhat of a mess as you may see in the papers. I sent to our bishop, Dr Ullathorne in Rome, one of the most confidential letters that I ever wrote in my life—and, without his fault, it got out and was shown about Rome.

Anxious as I am, I will not believe that the Pope's infallibility can be defined at the Council till I see it actually done. Certainly we, at least, have no claim to call ourselves infallible. Still it is our duty to act as if we were, and to leave the event to God. That is right, isn't it?

In the fatal letter to Ullathorne Newman had written:

Suddenly there is thunder in the clear sky. No impending danger is
to be averted but a great difficulty is to be created. Is this the proper
work for an Ecumenical Council? When has definition of doctrine
de fide been a luxury of devotion and not a stern painful necessity?

That was a fine restatement of his general position, of the
'inopportunist' view. But what caught the eye of the press was a
reference immediately afterwards to "an aggressive and insolent
faction" and "a clique of Jesuits, Redemptorists and Converts".

Little wonder that Manning felt himself the object of Newman's
reproach, even if he was not personally named, for Manning had
become the the driving force behind the scenes at Rome. Soon
enough, on 18 July 1870, the decree on Papal Infallibility was passed
by an overwhelming majority.

Tom Mozley, Harriet's widower, had resigned his living as a
country vicar, moved to London, and become a leader-writer for *The
Times*. He vividly described the scene in St Peter's.

Now there was a lull broken at last by the shrill voice of the
Secretary reading the Dogma, followed by the roll-call of the
Fathers. And *Placet* after *Placet* followed, uttered in louder
and bolder tones than on former occasions, and amid these
utterances there was a loud peal of thunder.

The storm was at its height when the result of the vote was taken
up to the Pope and the darkness was so thick that a huge taper was
necessarily brought and placed by his side as he read the words.

I was standing at the moment in the south transept when
the sound of a mighty rushing something caused me to start
violently. It grew and swelled—a cloud of white handkerchiefs
waving before me. *Viva il Papa Infallibile!* shouted the zealots.

The *Te Deum* and the benedictions, however, put a stop
to it. The entire crowd fell on their knees as I have never seen
a crowd do before in St Peter's and the Pope blessed them in
those clear sweet tones distinguishable among a thousand.

Rome had been full of the Catholic aristocracy, old and new, for the council. Acton, living in splendour with his young wife and two little daughters in the Palazzo Chigi— he had married a Bavarian cousin, much to the disappointment of many Catholic matriarchs with girls to dispose of—was created a peer of the realm, the first Baron Acton, by Queen Victoria while in Rome, on the recommendation, of course, of her new(ish) prime minister, Mr Gladstone. It, and Gladstone's support, and his own febrile canvassing, availed the liberal cause nothing against that other Englishman, by his opponents nicknamed *il diavolo del Concilio*. Acton left before the vital vote. But he never left the Church—unlike the great Dr Döllinger, who was to be publicly excommunicated the following year for his persistent and open refusal to accept the defined dogma.

Many of the bold young sprigs of the Catholic aristocracy had joined the Papal Zouaves to defend Rome. But with the almost immediate outbreak of the Franco-Prussian War, the professional soldiers of the French garrison were withdrawn and the Zouaves' parents, wisely, returned to the safety of their English, Irish or Scottish country estates. Vittorio Emmanuele's troops advanced on the City. The British Zouaves drank wine in the Café Greco, and swore to die in defence of their pope.

But Pio Nono, being sweet-natured as well as sweet-toned, wisely ordered his young and barely trained Zouaves to surrender. He himself retreated behind the Vatican walls with his Swiss Guards as the victorious atheistic House of Savoy seized the Eternal City and all its *palazzi,* and proudly proclaimed the Kingdom of United Italy. Shipped back to Liverpool, the woebegone and bedraggled Zouaves were entertained to a great consolatory dinner by that immensely rich, and immensely young, Christ Church-undergraduate-convert (not one of Newman's), the Marquess of Bute.

The spiritual power of the papacy had been strengthened, but the Temporal Power was totally extinguished—if not for ever at least up to and into the twenty-first century.

It was amazing, in the end and after all the fierce, divisive, embittered controversy, how little difference in practice either of these apparently momentous changes were to make.

Not that that was how people felt at the time. Quite the contrary indeed; and the one, possibly, who most felt the contrary was none other than the prime minister, Mr Gladstone.

Gladstone had been prime minister since 1868, and been occupied, naturally enough, with myriad matters. In March 1873 the Irish had scuppered his Irish University Bill, a complicated new proposal in which Newman had wisely refused to get involved (on the grounds of being totally out of touch), and Gladstone had resigned. But politics and resignations and new prime ministers are not always a simple thing in complex situations. Mr Disraeli refused to take office; the constitutional position was much argued; and Gladstone had to stay on, grumpily, until a General Election in February 1874 gave Disraeli and the Tories an absolutely clear mandate—a fifty-seat majority over all other parties combined, Liberals and Irish alike.

On 17 February Mr Gladstone went down to Windsor to hand in his resignation. His defeat, he told Queen Victoria, had been "the greatest expression of public disapprobation of a Government which he ever remembered." He intended to quit politics, as "wrangling" in the House of Commons was not "a fit thing for people in old age". Little did he, or the queen, or anyone, think that in the next twenty years he would again be prime minister, not once, not twice, but no fewer than three more times.

Be that as it may, in early 1874 he was bitter, disillusioned, ageing, with a grievance against the Irish (for whom he had tried to do so much[3]) and with time on his hands. So first he read Archbishop Manning's recent pamphlet on *Caesarism and Ultramontanism*, which, with its attack on the first and support for the second, put him in an even worse mood, and then, in the autumn, he travelled.

He went to Munich to see his old friend Dr Döllinger. That did not improve his temper, either. "It makes my blood run cold," he wrote to Mrs Gladstone, "to think of his being excommunicated in his venerable but, thank God, hale and strong old age. I know no one with whose mode of viewing and handling religious matters I

---

3 There was a feeling that the Vatican was behind the defeat of Gladstone's Irish University Bill though Manning told the prime minister: "It is not your fault or the Bill's fault"—he had tried to persuade Archbishop Cullen to support it—"but the fault of England and Scotland and three anti-Catholic centuries." Hardly consoling or even very tactful.

more cordially agree." He also took the opportunity to summon his sister Helen, now living in Germany, and attempt, unsuccessfully, to reconvert her to the Anglican fold. She further disconcerted him by out-walking him—29 miles in one day.

It seems fair to say that it was a thoroughly grumpy Gladstone who, back in England, wrote for the October issue of the *Contemporary Review* an article entitled "Ritualism and Ritual" which condemned Rome for bringing about in 1870—i.e. in the declaration of papal infallibility—"a policy of violence and change in faith" so that "no one can become her convert without renouncing his mental and moral freedom."

Naturally enough all converts, Newman included, took this badly. And this was to be only the first blast of the former prime minister's trumpet. He was preparing a much longer pamphlet, of 74 pages, to be published, deliberately it seems, on Guy Fawkes' Day, with the long-winded title of *The Vatican Decrees and their Bearing on Civil Allegiance: A Political Expostulation*—of which the gist was that no Roman Catholic could henceforward be a loyal citizen because the pope now had the infallible power to issue orders willy-nilly, which all Roman Catholics must obey.

Ambrose Phillipps was at Hawarden, and he put it to Gladstone that Newman should look over the text of the *Expostulation* "from a moderate (Catholic) point of view". Gladstone made it clear that he did not want to communicate with Newman directly, but allowed Ambrose Phillipps to send Newman the proofs—a courteous gesture but in practice a meaningless one since Newman only received the proofs on 6 November, a day after publication.

The *Expostulation* was an immediate success. It sold 150,000 copies. In its sixpenny edition it blanketed England. It made Gladstone an enormous £2,000 in royalties (and allowed him to keep his London house). And, morally, it seemed to be triumphant.

"That the Roman Catholic Church has brought itself into direct and visible antagonism with civil allegiance throughout the world," proclaimed *The Times,* "has now become unquestionable." To Newman it seemed that the *Expostulation* contained "some very unjustifiable cruel things. I fear," he wrote to Ambrose Phillipps, "we shall have great difficulty in making everything clear and satisfactory to the Protestant mind."

But the Catholics of England tried. They tried with a bravado and enthusiasm among the clergy that nowadays almost beggars belief. In less than a fortnight Bishop Ullathorne had produced a pamphlet entitled *The Döllingerites and Apostates from the Faith* (to be followed, later, by a whole book, *Mr Gladstone's Expostulations Unravelled*). Bishop Clifford of Clifton issued a Pastoral. Bishop Vaughan of Salford[4] issued a Pastoral. Father Henry Coleridge—Jesuit, long-time editor of *The Month* and convert son of that Mr Justice Coleridge who had so long ago sentenced Newman for criminal libel—preached a famous sermon on "The Abomination of Desolation". And Archbishop Manning prepared a 193-page-long enormous counter-attack on his old friend's outpourings entitled *The Vatican Decrees in their Bearing on Civil Allegiance*.

Yet all these, admirable though they were as gestures, were almost irrelevant. All eyes were on the English Catholics' one great writer: Newman.

The Duke of Norfolk wrote, urging Newman to reply. The duke, still only 26, was a solemn young man who would one day become the first Mayor of Westminster as well as Lord Mayor of Sheffield (and, rather more grandly, Earl Marshal of England and preside at two coronations). But already he was known as a "model chairman" and, of course, he was the leading Catholic layman and peer.

Newman agreed to reply. Indeed, he was already working on the reply. He had been working five to six hours a day without much result throughout November (owing to the "rambling and slovenly" nature of Gladstone's arguments which made it difficult to reply with "any logical exactness")—"I did nothing else than write all day; and every morning simply pluck every page I had written the day before and begin again"—until on 23 November "life seemed to come into me of a sudden and from that day I wrote straight off without stopping"—very much as he had done for the *Apologia*.

---

4 Who was to be Manning's successor and the third Archbishop of Westminster. An Old Catholic, all five of his sisters became nuns and six of his seven brothers priests.

That was in a letter to Dean Church. To the duke he wrote very differently, simply asking whether the reply might be addressed to him. Flattered, but rather shy, the duke wondered whether it should not be addressed directly to Mr Gladstone. "I am too old," Newman replied, "to stand up to my man as a champion. I am too old to give my opinion unasked when no duty compels me." The duke accepted, "with great happiness". And so on 14 June 1875, appeared *A Letter*— of ten chapters and 131 pages—*Addressed to His Grace the Duke of Norfolk on Occasion of Mr Gladstone's Recent Expostulation.*

The *Letter* was an immediate triumph. In his *Expostulation* Gladstone had been on occasions wildly abusive. He had referred to "the myrmidons of the apostolic chambers", to papal claims "like hideous mummies picked out of Egyptian sarcophagi", to the design of re-erecting the Temporal Power "even if it could only be re-erected on the ashes of the city, and amidst the whitening bones of the people." In reply the *Letter* was courteous in tone, even if at times silkily courteous. And not only the press but Gladstone himself acknowledged its vast superiority. "You may from the newspapers perceive," wrote the vanquished to the victor, "that yesterday was a busy day for me, for I had to fold my mantle and to die."

Newman for his part could not have been further from triumphalism, even though his triumph was virtually[5] complete. "It has been a great grief to me," he most graciously wrote to Mr Gladstone (whose political career he assumed, like everyone else, to be over—he may soon be a saint but he was certainly no prophet) "to have had to write against one whose career I have followed from first to last with so much (I may say) loyal interest and admiration."

I had looked at you with kindly curiosity, before you came up to Christ Church. From the time you were launched into public life you have retained a hold on my thoughts and my

---

5 Virtually, because Gladstone nonetheless went on immediately to write a second pamphlet of 120 pages entitled *Vaticanismus: An Answer to Replies and Reproofs*; to which Newman rejoined with a 24-page *Postcript* to the *Letter*—both published in February 1875. But *Vaticanismus* did not catch on in the same way as the *Expostulation* had (nor did the term itself, derived from Dr Döllinger's Vatikanismus). Gladstone was reduced to consoling himself with "a letter of thanks from Bismarck," the Prussian Chancellor, then about to launch (much incidentally, to Döllinger's dismay) the totally anti-Christian *Kulturkampf*.

gratitude. What a fate it is that now when so memorable a career has reached its formal termination, I should be the man to present to you, amid the many expressions of public sympathy which it elicits, a controversial pamphlet as my offering.

"I do not think I can ever be sorry for what I have done, but I can never cease to be sorry," came the elegant ending, "for the necessity of doing it."

Gladstone was to outlive both Newman and Döllinger, and pay tributes to both of them in his late-life letters to Acton (most warmly to Döllinger, of course). "I think nine-tenths of my intercourse with him was oral, with Cardinal Newman nothing like one-tenth. In D's case it was very precious." But though "Ever since Newman published his University Sermons in 1843 I have thought him unsafe in philosophy," Gladstone concluded: "he was a wonderful man, a holy man, a very refined man and (to me) a most kindly man."

The *Letter* was almost immediately translated into German, under the title of *Ist die Katholische Kirche staatsgefährlich?* (presumably both to Dr Döllinger's and Prince Bismarck's dismay) and soon, like Newman's revived fame, spread itself worldwide. There are three points about it that must be made.

The first is that it easily and completely rebuts (from its very first sentence onwards) "The main question which Mr Gladstone has started [which] I take to be this: Can Catholics be trustworthy subjects of the State? Has not a foreign power a hold over their consciences such, that it may at any time be used to the serious perplexity and injury of the civil government under which they live?" Newman disposes of this by explaining, carefully and logically, the limits of the doctrine of papal infallibility. There is a whole chapter devoted to *The Vatican Definition* of which the following two extracts will give a flavour.

Neither in conversation, nor in discussion, nor in interpreting Scripture or the Fathers, nor in consulting, nor in giving reasons for the point which he has defined, nor in answering letters, nor in private deliberations, supposing he is setting forth his own opinions, is the Pope infallible.

And:

> His infallibility in consequence is not called into exercise, unless he speaks to the whole world; for, if his precepts, in order to be dogmatic, must enjoin what is necessary to salvation, they must be necessary for all men. Accordingly orders which issue from him for the observance of particular countries, or political or religious classes, have no claim to be the utterances of infallibility. If he enjoins upon the hierarchy of Ireland to withstand mixed education, this is no exercise of his infallibility.

Newman probably enjoyed penning that last sentence, both for Gladstone's sake and his own. What he also undoubtedly enjoyed was pointing out, indirectly, to the ultra-Ultramontanes that the definition of infallibility was in the end far more limited than that much wider dogma for which they had hoped.

And it worked. Even W.G. Ward, that ultra of ultras, praised him[6] and the *Letter* in the *Dublin Review* that April, and Manning wrote to a worried Propaganda that "the substance of the *Letter* was sound" and should in no circumstances be condemned—though one can understand why Propaganda were worried that in such a detailed analysis Newman might at some point have veered away on a totally unorthodox tack.

Instead—and this is point two—it could be said that modern critics, Catholic and Protestant alike, have veered away on a totally wrong tack. They have taken the famous ending of the chapter on *Conscience* where Newman writes: "Certainly, if I am obliged to bring religion into after-dinner toasts (which indeed does not seem quite the thing) I shall drink—to the Pope, if you please,—still, to Conscience first, and to the Pope afterwards" all on its own, as if it were not preceded by ten pages of fairly dense argument, particularly as to "the notion of conscience in this day in the popular mind", which does not seem to have changed in this past 150 years.

---

6 Since their break, wrote a deeply emotional Ward to Newman, he had become a "kind of intellectual orphan".

When men advocate the rights of conscience, they in no sense mean the rights of the Creator nor the duty to him of the creature; but the right of thinking, speaking, writing and acting according to their judgement or their humour, without any thought of God at all.

They do not even pretend to go by any moral rule, but they demand what they think is an Englishman's prerogative, for each to be his master in all things, and to profess what he pleases, asking no one's leave.

Conscience has rights because it has duties; but in this age, with a large portion of the public it is the very right and duty of conscience to dispense with conscience.

It becomes a licence to take up any or no religion, to take up this or that and let it go again, to go to church, to go to chapel, to boast of being above all religions and to be an impartial critic of each of them.

Conscience is a stern monitor, but in this century it has been superseded by a counterfeit, which the eighteen centuries prior to it never heard of, and could not have mistaken for it, if they had.

So Newman, in the *Letter*, distinguishes most markedly the "counterfeit conscience", which he, and the Church of the Ages, utterly condemn. How many of us can honestly say, in all good conscience, that ours is not a counterfeit conscience as defined above?

The third and final point is this: and again it is best served by a quotation. Again and again there had been rumours that Newman was poorly appreciated by, and therefore dissatisfied with, his "new" Church; and was considering returning to his "old", original fold. Poorly appreciated, yes, in some quarters. Dissatisfied with, yes, occasionally. But as the *Postscript* to the *Letter* puts it:

All I can say, in answer to it, is that from the day I became a Catholic to this day, now close upon thirty years, I have never had a moment's misgiving that the communion of Rome is that Church which the Apostles set up at Pentecost and in which the Anglican communion, whatever its merits and demerits, whatever the great excellence of individuals in it, has, as such, no part.

On 15 March 1885 the Archbishop of Westminster, summoned to Rome for the occasion, was at last created a cardinal. Pio Nono had not forgotten Manning's great speech in favour of infallibility at the Vatican Council five years earlier. The Duke of Norfolk raised £6500 as a gift from the laity to enable the new cardinal to keep up appearances. Minna his mother, the dowager duchess, wrote from Arundel Castle that "I think there are few who have rejoiced with a keener and more personal joy than I have done"; and from the Birmingham Oratory on Easter Eve Newman wrote to "My dear Lord Cardinal" offering "the sincere prayer of yours affectionately" and noting, appositely enough,

> As regards the Protestant world, it is striking to observe the contrast between the circumstances under which you are invested with this special dignity, and the feelings which were excited in England twenty-five years ago on occasion of the like elevation of your predecessor, Cardinal Wiseman.

But for Newman there were no new honours; only an event, that same spring, of great pain.

Father Ambrose St John was a lynchpin not only of Newman's life, as he had been ever since those days at Littlemore, but of the Birmingham Oratory. He ran the school, he ran the Altar Society, he was the chief administrator—the Father Minister. He had arranged to buy Ravenhurst Farm, 1½ miles away from the oratory, for its playing-fields, and had set up a chapel in the conservatory there. He was translating theology from the German for Newman. He was immensely hard-working. He would turn sixty that June. He was indispensable.

One of Newman's passions was putting on Latin plays with the schoolboys of the Oratory School. He cut them enormously down to about half an hour of performance, preferring Terence to Plautus and, of course, censoring the bawdiness to the taste of the times. He even eventually published four of them in his collected works, in both Latin and English versions: three plays of Terence (including the *Phormio*) and one of Plautus, *ad usum puerorum* as his inscription ran.

The first sign that something was very wrong was when Ambrose St John interrupted Newman at his work in an over-excited frame of mind to discuss, for almost an hour, the boys' costumes for the current Latin play. That was in April. In early May, walking home from Ravenhurst Farm, he apparently had a touch of sunstroke and nearly collapsed. On Ascension Day, 6 May, he said Mass as usual, seemed fine, but later began rambling, reminding Newman that the pope had called him "Newman's Baronius". He was placed in the sick-room but thought he was being sent to the lunatic asylum.[7] First an ordinary doctor was called, then a specialist. He was taken on doctor's orders to Ravenhurst Farm to rest and recuperate. From 9 May to 15 May was his "wild time" —shouting, whimpering, fears he was being poisoned. At one moment he had to be tied to his bed. The doctors diagnosed "brain fever". It all sounds quite ghastly.

Then he seemed to recover. The doctor was optimistic but Newman was not. Ambrose's speech was still slurred and inconsequent. "Through the morning he kept speaking to us, but we could not understand a word he said. This was very painful; he was not excited at all; at times he pointed at the window as if he saw something there."

On the evening of 24 May with Newman sitting beside him, he ate some bread and butter. At 7pm Newman left for the oratory saying he would see him "better still tomorrow morning". At midnight there was a knocking on his bedroom door. Father Ambrose, he was told, was much worse.

In fact he was already dead. He had died quite suddenly after putting himself to bed in the presence of Father William Neville, the infirmarian, at a quarter to eleven. It was well after midnight therefore when Newman reached Ravenhurst Farm, and an hour later he was

---

7 The Fathers of the Birmingham Oratory, including of course St John, had recently heard that Dalgairns of the London Oratory had shown ever-increasing signs of "mental disturbance", and I imagine was probably in some sort of asylum—so St John's apprehension was natural enough.

saying Mass for the repose of his friend and companion's soul in the conservatory that Ambrose St John had converted into a chapel.

Newman publicly broke down at the Requiem when he was giving Absolution. To Emily Bowles he wrote on 2 June a long account of the illness and death. "I must read it over before I send it to you. A day does not pass without my having violent outbursts of crying, and they weaken me, and I dread them. Also I wish"—and this seems typical of Newman, a man in whom emotion and intellect were almost always in equipoise—"Father William to cast his eye over what I have written to see if I am correct."

Newman was in his seventies now, and other old friends were falling off their perches at an alarming and saddening rate—Henry Wilberforce a particular loss. But there were new recruits to the Birmingham Oratory, a spate of new novices, so that its survival, and that of the school, seemed assured. Indeed, Newman's successor as superior was to be Father Ignatius Ryder, son of George Ryder and of the last of the beautiful Miss Sargents, he whose parents had been given a house by Ambrose Phillipps on the Grace Dieu Estate, he whose beautiful aunt had once been Cardinal Manning's (as he then was not) wife…

Pio Nono too was dying, was on his deathbed in the Vatican. *Non videbis dies Petri* they had sung, traditionally, at his coronation with the Triple Crown. No longer could it be sung, for he had far outlived the traditional twenty-five years of the Primacy of Peter. *Addio carissimo*, he said to Cardinal Manning who knelt by his deathbed and kissed his hand. It truly was the end of an era, of the longest papacy ever. He died in the early afternoon of Thursday 8 February 1878.

The Sacred College of Cardinals, seventy strong at the time, met in conclave on Monday 18 February to elect a new pope. Manning's name was among those put forward; he received two votes. An Italian was, of course, elected: Cardinal Pecci of Perugia was unknown to Manning, and Manning to him. Elected on Wednesday 20th on the third ballot he took the name and title of Leo XIII. Leo XIII was a man of 68, a moderate traditionalist, unlike his predecessor in that he was open to intellectuals and interested in scholarship.

It was a woeful time for Newman, lonely, unproductive, nearly ten years older than the new pope, still vaguely under a cloud, or so he thought, in Rome.

In the history of English Catholicism it is amazing, but encouraging, how often the laity have stepped in, brusquely, effectively, where the clergy have hung back. It happened in Bishop Challoner's time when he was all for a quiet life and no troubling of the status quo. Now, a hundred years later it was to happen again.

The Duke of Norfolk had been a founder member, in 1870, of the Catholic Union, which under his presidency quickly became the leading body of Catholic laymen in England. The young duke's determination, whatever his shyness, should not be underestimated. It was he who stepped in to save the English College when the new Italian kingdom had confiscated it and the British government had washed its hands of all pleas. He bought it personally at auction for 59,000 lira. To the duke on publication of the *Letter* Newman had courteously written: "It will be a great satisfaction to me, in the last thing probably I shall write, to end my say with the great House of Norfolk on my tongue." And indeed, the *Letter* was in effect the last thing of importance that Newman was to write.

The duke did not forget the ageing and half forgotten recluse at Birmingham. At the beginning of the new pontificate the Catholic Union bestirred itself. A deputation—the duke himself, that elder statesman, future Viceroy of India (and convert) the Marquess of Ripon and Lord Petre—waited on Cardinal Manning. In effect, politely but firmly, they recommended that Dr Newman's enormous services should at last be officially recognised. In a long letter[8] the duke explained his motives:

I was moved very much by the feeling that it was due to Newman himself that his long life of marvellous and

8 Written to Newman's first biographer, William Ward, the son of W.G. Ward; and to be found (for those interested) almost in its entirety in his second volume. It was William's daughter, W.G.'s granddaughter Maisie Ward, whose *Young Mr Newman* filled the early-year gaps her father's biography had left. Thus three generations of Wards focused on Newman.

successful labour for religion should receive the highest mark of recognition which the Holy See could give him.

I felt this all the more keenly because I knew how much had happened to obscure the character of the work he had done.

I know that it must be an intense sorrow to him to feel that he and his life's work were not understood in that very quarter of which he had made himself the special champion.

But my chief reason was based on more general grounds. I do not think that any Catholic has been listened to by those who are not Catholics with so much attention, respect, and, to great extent, sympathy as Newman.

True then, true now.

Manning bent his head in silence for a few long moments, then agreed to draft a letter to Rome proposing "the elevation of Dr Newman to the Sacred College." This was in August 1878.

There were delays and hiccups, and the duke himself had to go to Rome and demand an audience with Pope Leo XIII where he put, and pressed, the case.

Newman was both delighted—"profoundly touched and moved" as Bishop Ullathrone put it—and dismayed. Dismayed because he did not wish, at his age, to leave *nidulo suo*, his little nest, and move to Rome. Misunderstandings followed. It took once again the Catholic Union's strong intervention to scotch the rumour that Dr Newman had rejected a cardinal's hat. The pope agreed without hesitation to Newman remaining in Birmingham. And an overjoyed, highly emotional old man declared to his brother priests at the oratory: "The cloud is lifted from me for ever."

By March 1879 he was writing exultantly to Dean Church (among myriad other replies to letters of congratulation): *"Haec mutatio dexterae Excelsi!* All the stories which have gone about of my being a half-Catholic, a Liberal Catholic, under a cloud, not to be trusted, are now at an end."

Newman, with Father William Neville to look after him, left for Rome on Easter Wednesday. They arrived at the City on Thursday 24 April. Newman took to his bed with a sore throat but was up on Sunday for an audience with the pope. "The Holy Father received me most affectionately." He asked many questions, including, rather sweetly, about the cooking arrangements at the oratory. "He has a clear white complexion—his eyes somewhat bloodshot. He speaks very slowly and clearly and with an Italian manner."

Newman and Neville moved to the Palazzo della Pigna, the residence of Cardinal Howard, the duke's cousin. There on Monday morning 12 May 1879, a messenger arrived bearing a *biglietto* from the Cardinal Secretary of State informing him that in a Consistory held that morning his Holiness had raised Dr Newman to the dignity of an eminence, a Prince of the Church.

The palazzo was crowded with ambassadors, bishops, the English of Rome, the "black" (papal) aristocracy. The messenger handed the *biglietto* to Newman who broke the seal, and Dr Clifford, Bishop of Clifton, read the contents. It was announced that his Holiness would receive the new cardinal at the Vatican at ten o'clock the following morning to confer the *biretta*, the Red Hat, upon him. And then, to the assembled multitude, Newman made his famous *biglietto* speech.

I am aware that, like all who write on Newman, I have picked and chosen (and indeed shortened) quotations from his works; one can hardly do otherwise. But in this particular case, I propose to give the *biglietto* speech in full so that no readers can feel that anything in it has been taken out of context. For this is the context, and a fittingly final one. It seems to me to echo in a nutshell—particularly in those sentences or paragraphs marked (here) in bold—all that Newman had stood for, consistently, throughout his adult life.

The new cardinal delivered, it was reported, "a very fine speech. How he managed it St Philip knows best—but he did not cough—and his delivery was very animated and perfect", ending "with the motto which is in the *Lives of the Saints* he published at Littlemore":

> The meek-spirited shall possess the earth
> And shall be refreshed in the multitude of peace.

Vi ringrazio, Monsignore, per la participazione che m'avete fatto dell' alto onore che il Santo Padre si è degnato conferire sulla mia umile persona.

And if I ask your permission to continue my address to you, not in your musical language, but in my own dear mother tongue, it is because in the latter I can better express my feelings on this most gracious announcement which you have brought to me than if I attempted what is above me.

First of all then, I am led to speak of the wonder and profound gratitude which came upon me, and which is upon me still, at the condescension and love towards me of the Holy Father, in singling me out for so immense an honour. It was a great surprise. Such an elevation had never come into my thoughts, and seemed to be out of keeping with all my antecedents. I had passed through many trials, but they were over; and now the end of all things had almost come to me, and I was at peace. And was it possible that after all I had lived through so many years for this?

Nor is it easy to see how I could have borne so great a shock, had not the Holy Father resolved on a second act of condescension towards me, which tempered it, and was to all who heard of it a touching evidence of his kindly and generous nature. He felt for me, and he told me the reasons why he raised me to this high position. Besides other words of encouragement, he said his act was a recognition of my zeal and good service for so many years in the Catholic cause; moreover, he judged it would give pleasure to English Catholics, and even to Protestant England, if I received some mark of his favour. After such gracious words from his Holiness, I should have been insensible and heartless if I had had scruples any longer.

This is what he had the kindness to say to me, and what could I want more? In a long course of years I have made many mistakes. I have nothing of that high perfection which belongs to the writings of saints, viz., that error cannot be found in them; but what I trust that I may claim all through what I have written, is this,—an honest intention, an absence of private ends, a temper of obedience, a willingness to be corrected, a dread of error, a desire to serve Holy Church, and, through Divine mercy, a fair measure of success. And, I rejoice to say, to one great mischief, I have from the first opposed myself. **For thirty, forty, fifty years I have resisted to the best of my powers the spirit of Liberalism in religion. Never did Holy Church need champions against it more sorely than now, when, alas! it is an error overspreading, as a snare, the whole earth;** and on this great occasion, when it is natural for one who is in my place to look out upon the world, and upon Holy Church as in it, and upon her future, it will not, I hope be considered out of place, if I renew the protest against it which I have made so often.

Liberalism in religion is the doctrine that there is no positive truth in religion, but that one creed is as good as another, and this is the teaching which is gaining substance and force daily. It is inconsistent with any recognition of any religion, as true. It teaches that all are to be tolerated for all are matters of opinion. Revealed religion is not a truth, but a sentiment and a taste; not an objective fact, not miraculous; and it is the right of each individual to make it say just what strikes his fancy. Devotion is not necessarily founded on faith. Men may go to Protestant Churches and to Catholic, may get good from both and belong to neither. They may fraternise together in spiritual thoughts and feelings, without having any views at all of doctrines in common, or seeing the need of them. Since, then, religion is so personal a peculiarity and so private a possession, we must of necessity ignore it in the intercourse of man with man. If a man puts on a new religion every morning, what is that to you? It is as impertinent to think about a man's religion as about his sources of income or his management of his family. Religion is in no sense the bond of society.

Hitherto the civil power has been Christian. Even in countries separated from the Church as in my own, the dictum was in force, when I was young, that: "Christianity

was the law of the land." Now, everywhere that goodly framework of society, which is the creation of Christianity, is throwing off Christianity. The dictum to which I have referred, with a hundred others which followed upon it, is gone, or is going everywhere; and, by the end of the century unless the Almighty interferes, it will be forgotten. Hitherto, it has been considered that religion alone, with its supernatural sanctions, was strong enough to secure submission of the masses of our population to law and order; now the Philosophers and Politicians are bent on satisfying this problem without the aid of Christianity. Instead of the Church's authority and teaching, they would substitute first of all a universal and thoroughly secular education, calculated to bring home to every individual that to be orderly, industrious and sober is his personal interest. Then, for great working principles to take the place of religion for the use of the masses thus carefully educated, it provides—the broad fundamental ethical truths, of justice, benevolence, veracity and the like; proved experience; and those natural laws which exist and act spontaneously in society, and in social matters, whether physical or psychological; for instance, in government, trade, finance, sanitary experiments, and the intercourse of nations. As to Religion, it is a private luxury, which a man may have if he will; but which of course he must pay for, and which he must not obtrude upon others, or indulge in to their annoyance.

The general nature of this great apostasia is one and the same everywhere; but in detail, and in character, it varies in different countries. For myself, I would rather speak of it in my own country, which I know. There, I think it threatens to have a formidable success; though it is not easy to see what will be its ultimate issue. At first sight it might be thought that Englishmen are too religious for a movement which, on the continent, seems to be founded on infidelity; but the misfortune with us is, that, though it ends in infidelity as in other places, it does not necessarily arise out of infidelity. It must be recollected that the religious sects, which sprang up in England three centuries ago, and which are so powerful now, have ever been fiercely opposed to the Union of Church and State, and would advocate the unchristianising of the monarchy and all that belongs to it, under the notion that such a catastrophe would make Christianity much more pure and much more powerful. Next the liberal principle is forced on us from the necessity of the case. Consider what follows from the very fact of these many sects. They constitute the religion, it is supposed, of half the population; and, recollect, our mode of government is popular. Every dozen men taken at random whom you meet in the streets have a share in political power,—when you inquire into their forms of belief, perhaps they represent one or other of as many as seven religions; how we can they possibly act together in municipal or in national matters, if each insists on the recognition of his own religious denomination? All action would be at a deadlock unless the subject of religion was ignored. We cannot help ourselves. **And, thirdly, it must be borne in mind, that there is much in the liberalistic theory which is good and true; for example, not to say more, the precepts of justice, truthfulness, sobriety, self-command, benevolence, which, as I have already noted, are among its avowed principles, and the natural laws of society. It is not till we find that this array of principles is intended to supersede, to block out, religion, that we pronounce it to be evil. There never was a device of the Enemy so cleverly framed and with such promise of success.** And already it has answered to the expectations which have been formed of it. It is sweeping into its own ranks great numbers of able, earnest, virtuous men, elderly men of approved antecedents, young men with a career before them.

Such is the state of things in England, and it is well that it should be realised by all of us; but it must not be supposed for a moment that I am afraid of it. I lament it deeply, because I foresee that it may be the ruin of many souls; but I have no fear at all that it can really do aught of serious harm to the Word of God, to Holy Church, to our Almighty King, the Lion of the tribe of Judah, Faithful and True, **or to His Vicar on earth.** Christianity has been too often in what seemed deadly peril, that we should fear for it any new trial now. So far is certain; on the other hand, what is uncertain, and in these great contests commonly is uncertain, and what is commonly a great surprise, when it is witnessed, **is the particular mode by which, in the event, Providence rescues and saves His elect inheritance. Sometimes our enemy is turned into a friend; sometimes he is despoiled of that special virulence of evil which was so threatening; sometimes he falls to pieces of himself; sometimes he does just so much as is beneficial, and then is removed.** Commonly the Church has nothing more to do than to go on in her own proper duties, in confidence and peace; to stand still and to see the salvation of God.

Mansueti hereditabunt terram
Et delectabuntur in multitudine pacis.

Two comments: first I would ask readers to pick out a sentence here or there from those set in bold; and note how, quoted in isolation, it would totally contradict what Newman means to say. For instance, "Men may go to Protestant Churches and Catholic, may get good from both and belong to neither"—an example not of what Newman propounds but of an attitude that he utterly abhors. Or, later, "Religion is in no sense the bond of society"—exactly the position he is condemning. Hence everyone, scholars and non-scholars alike, need always to be very wary about accepting any short quotes from Newman at face value. The person putting them forward may, deliberately or not, be utterly traducing Newman's meaning.

Secondly, what would Newman make of the present-day ecumenical movement? It seems to me—as surely it must seem to all fair-minded readers on reading the *biglietto* speech—that, though recognising the good intentions and personal virtues of not only Anglicans and fellow-Christians but nowadays, no doubt, of Muslims, Hindus and Buddhists too, he would frankly and openly have condemned their religious beliefs as simply not being true.

As for liberalism: "There never was a device of the Enemy so cleverly framed and with such promise of success." That quotation, as readers will see for themselves, is not taken out of context, but is Newman's definitive conclusion. For Newman, liberalism is, like it or not, definitely pronounced "to be evil".

Intermezzo IV

Shuffling Off This Mortal Coil

The procession from Hagley Road to Rednal

Cardinal Newman had intended, on his journey home, to visit Dr Döllinger in Munich and Maria Giberne—now Sister Maria Pia—at Autun in France. But he was too weak and ill.

At Norfolk House in London later that summer there was a great two-day reception to celebrate. The doors were thrown open to Catholics, but not only to Catholics. In one day four hundred came: "I only know that the Duke slaved, nay the Duchess too." Gladstone did not come, nor indeed Manning. Newman saw the spires of Oxford closer once again, made an Honorary Fellow of the college of which he had been an undergraduate, Trinity, attended the College Gaudy there and preached in the new Jesuit Church of St Aloysius, which was destined a century later to become the Oxford Oratory—a consummation devoutly to be wished.

His sister Jemima died on Christmas Day 1879, still barely reconciled. On 5 January 1882 he wrote to Maria Giberne of his other, favourite, sister: "This is the anniversary of my dear Mary's death in 1828—an age ago; but she is as fresh in my memory and dear to my heart as if it were yesterday; and often I cannot mention her name without tears coming into my eyes."

General Gordon died in 1885 at Khartoum, unrescued—much to the country and the queen's disgust—by Gladstone. And to the cardinal's disgust too. "Neither the Crimea nor the Indian Mutiny has come home to me," he wrote to a female friend, "I don't know why, as this has. Perhaps it is because the misfortune is so wanton and on that ground makes one so indignant." He had maps of the Sudan pinned up on the walls of his room and would not allow them to be removed, even when Khartoum fell to the Mahdi. It was only later that he was to learn that Gordon, truly in arms against a sea of troubles, had had with him at Khartoum a copy of *The Dream of Gerontius* and had marked his favourite passages in pencil.

He made his last trip to London for the Requiem of Minna, dowager duchess of Norfolk, and there, on the steps of Brompton Oratory, the two eminences, Cardinal Manning and Cardinal Newman, met, very briefly, for the last time. Manning by now was an old man too.

By 1887: "I wish the state of my fingers allowed me to write ... My difficulty in writing breaks my thought ... My fingers"—this to Gerard Manley Hopkins in the letter quoted at the end of Intermezzo III—"will not let me write more", and to Dean Church, that summer: "For myself, though I have no complaint, *senectus ipsa est morbus*, showing itself in failure of sight, speech, joints, hearing." *Sans* eyes, *sans* ears—indeed the Seventh Age of Man.

He preached for the last time on 1 January 1888. "When we look back at the lives of holy men," he *inter alia* said, (and he was not referring to himself though we might now so apply it), "it often seems wonderful that God has not employed them more fully."

"It might be said of the Cardinal," wrote Father Neville, "that he clung to life to the end." Happily so, as his last visitor, on 9 August 1890, was his niece Grace, Harriet and Tom Mozley's only child, over from New Zealand, whom he had not seen since she was a little girl aged three at Littlemore, before his conversion and the rift with her mother. He held her hand, and she his.

That evening he seemed less frail. "The Cardinal entered his room, unbent, erect, without a support of any kind. His whole carriage was, it may be said, soldier-like; and his countenance was most attractive to look at. Even great age seemed to have gone from his face; and with it all careworn signs." Thus the faithful Father Neville.

Next day, though, 10 August, he received the Last Sacraments. On 11 August he was unconscious most of the day. The Fathers of the Oratory gathered around his bedside; and that evening might, with the Priest of Gerontius, have said:

Proficiscere, anima Christiana, de hoc mundo.
Go forth upon thy journey, Christian soul.
Go from this world! Go, in the name of God
Son of the living God, who bled for Thee!
Go, in the name of the Holy Spirit, who
Hath been poured out on thee! Go, in the name
Of Angels and Archangels; in the name
Of Thrones and Dominations; in the name
Of Princedoms and of Powers; and in the name
Of Cherubim and Seraphim, go forth!
Go, in the name of Patriarchs and Prophets;
And of Apostles and Evangelists,
Of Martyrs and Confessors; in the name
Of holy Monks and Hermits; in the name
Of holy Virgins and all Saints of God.

So they might have chanted as at a quarter to nine that evening the Soul of the Old Man in his ninetieth year quitted this earth with the thought, perhaps, that

> I went to sleep; and now I am refreshed
> A strange refreshment; for I feel in me
> An inexpressive lightness... How still it is

and was escorted, by his Angel, straight up to be enrolled among "all Saints of God".

The Birmingham Oratory fronts the Hagley Road—a cavernous Victorian building, on the border line between leafy Edgbaston and the "black country" (now used in both senses) of Ladywood. Behind it lie the now-empty buildings of the Oratory School.[1] Beside it, set back a little, is the beautiful extravagant neo-baroque church. In front of the church is a cloister-like courtyard; and set on one wall of

---

1 The Oratory School moved, between the wars, to outside Reading—and much more spacious grounds—where it still flourishes.

the courtyard are 33 memorial plaques—one for each of the Fathers of the Oratory who have died there.

At the top, about three times the size of the others, surmounted by his coat-of-arms (of three hearts) and his famous motto, *Cor ad cor loquitur*, is the cardinal's memorial plaque. Directly below is that of his faithful attendant, Father Neville, with the inscription: "*Orate Pro Anima Patris Gulielmi Neville Obit 15 Mar 1905. Aet 80*". All the other plaques including the cardinal's own are similarly concise and to the point.

All except three. These are slightly larger than the rest—about three feet long, eighteen inches high—and adorned with much more fervent Latin inscriptions. There are the three plaques of the Fathers of the Oratory who died before Newman, and the tributes are obviously composed by Newman himself. To Ambrose St John, stressing his headmastership of the school; to Father Joseph Gordon, who died aged only forty: *Dulcissima Anima - Lepidum, Humanum, Amabilem*; and above all to Father Edward Caswall, a wealthy widower who joined the Oratory in 1852 and died there aged 64. It was his money, and the legacy that came to him from his wife, about £10,000 in all, that basically built the church and the Oratory itself: *Benefactoris Singularis* as Newman rightly wrote, *In Vita Amabilis, In Morte Flebilis*.

These are the three whom Newman was determined to be as close to in death as he was in life. At the little green cemetery , out at Rednal, where rows of Celtic crosses mark the graves of the Fathers, all plain and equal and unadorned, Newman was buried with Father Gordon's grave on one side, Father Caswell's on the other, and Father St John's coffin below his own. It is a quiet peaceful spot, at the foot of the Lickey Hills, the Fathers' country retreat in what was then a hamlet way outside Birmingham.[2]

---

2 Rednal, rather a fine house with, at one side, its own vaulted chapel (designed by John Hungerford Pollen) is now, past desolate Longbridge, on the outer edge of Birmingham. Old Oscott (Maryvale) and New Oscott are both swallowed up by northern Birmingham— though New Oscott, the seminary, has extensive grounds giving it still a country feel. Pugin's Cathedral, St Chad's, is isolated on a major road surrounded by the hideous 1960s redevelopments of Birmingham centre.

"A leader is fallen in Israel, and with him passes away one of the greatest Englishmen, and beyond all question the greatest master of the English language of our time." That is how Newman's death was reported in the *Manchester Guardian*, not a natural supporter. The wording is typical enough of the tone of the now-legendary 1500 obituaries that were to appear in the press worldwide.

The funeral itself took place on Tuesday 19 August 1890. No fewer than seventeen bishops attended the Requiem Mass in, as the *Birmingham Post* reported, full canonicals and "with a pomp which personally he would have eschewed". Bishop Clifford—the same who had read the *biglietto* out on that great occasion in Rome—preached the funeral sermon, and at the end of the service the coffin, placed in a glass hearse, was followed by twelve carriages along the seven miles out to Rednal. "An immense crowd" went the report, "filled the Hagley Road and lined the route—the Highfield Road, the Priory Road and the Bristol Road. A large number of persons followed the procession in omnibuses and breaks to Rednal and many hundreds of people on foot accompanied it a long way on its journey."

"He was laid to rest with an absence, so far as the obsequies at Rednal were concerned, of all pomp and show. This is the resting place he chose for himself years ago when he was plain John Henry Newman. He was there as lately as June last and looked long upon the grave which now he shares. It lies between two other graves of priests of the Oratory—those of Father Edward Caswall who died in 1878 and Father Joseph Gordon who died in 1853."

And there the earthly remains of John Henry rested undisturbed for nearly 120 years until on 2 October 2008 they were exhumed. This is a normal procedure [as the next chapter will indicate] when a Catholic is to be beatified or canonised. Sometimes the body is found uncorrupted. The Fathers of the Oratory and the representatives of the Birmingham Archdiocesan Tribunal apparently half expected to find a lead-lined coffin, with its well preserved contents. So did the man from the Ministry of Justice who, obligatorily, attended—one cannot go about exhuming bodies in England, even bodies of possible saints, without considerable paperwork and official authorisations.

They were disappointed. They should have studied more carefully the long article in the *Birmingham Post*, which concludes:

> When the rites had been achieved, the crowd without the gates was suffered to enter by batches and see the grave; and then the coffin was covered with mould of a softer texture than the marly stratum in which the grave is cut.
>
> This was done in studious and affectionate fulfilment of a desire of Dr Newman's which some may deem fanciful, but which sprang from his reverence for the letter of the Divine Word; which, as he conceived it, enjoins us to facilitate rather than impede the operation of the law:
>
> 'Dust thou art, and unto dust shalt thou return."

So of the bones and flesh of Cardinal Newman, indeed of his wooden un-lead-lined coffin, only dust remained. All that was exhumed was the brass plate on the coffin, which did at least fulfil one requirement, that of identifying the grave as being the last resting place, genuinely, of the candidate for beatification, the servant of God. And a small amount of unidentifiable material—part perhaps of the robe.

Both are preserved, together with the cardinal's vestments and those many other ornate robes about the expense of purchasing which he had bitterly complained, and which he had so rarely worn, in his little room on the first floor of the Birmingham Oratory, with its tiny ornate cardinal's chapel at the side—and the writing desk at which he stood to toss off, in that great fever of creativity, the *Apologia*.

But of bones, heart, fingers, hair—only dust remain.

Chapter Seven

Beatification and Beyond

Benedict XVI: the Pope of the Beatification

Is it fair to say that ever since 1559 the English in general have been suspicious of saints, miracles, canonisation, beatification, devils' advocates, postulators, causes and all the rest of it? Or if not exactly suspicious of, at least uneasy with? And baffled by? Understandably. For I too, an Englishman, as I have tried to understand in these recent months, have been much baffled—and the more so, the deeper one probes.

I take 1559 as the cut-off point because that was when in effect the government of the day virtually abolished saints in England. The Act of Uniformity, passed by a knife-edge three votes in the first House of Commons of Elizabeth's reign, put an end to a generation of religious to-ings and fro-ings under two kings and two queens. In the next years statues, wall-paintings in churches, stained glass windows, processions, chapels, pretty much everything to do with saints (except names and days) were pulled down, whitewashed over, smashed, condemned, abandoned and ridiculed. From then on saints were, essentially, out.

But before that—and not all that long before—how very different it was. Every English village, town, guild, and trade had its patron saint. Saints were God's friends indeed but everyone else's friends and helpers too. *The Golden Legend* gives six reasons for venerating saints: first to honour God, for "who that doth honour to saints, he honoureth Him specially which sanctified them." Secondly—and this is what attracted most people—"for aid in our infirmity", and thirdly, as a famous preacher put it summing up, for their "high holynes of lyvying".

How times change! Attentive readers will have spotted that phrase in Newman's *biglietto* speech where he says: "At first sight it might be thought that Englishmen are too religious for... (etc., etc.)." Englishmen too religious! How extraordinarily improbable that now sounds. And now, on 19 September, Newman himself is to be made a saint (or, to be precise, a Blessed) by the pope in person—certainly the most important English saint since the Reformation, since 1559. What does it all mean?

I think the only way to understand all this, to reduce it from gibberish to comprehension (and as much for Catholics as for non-Catholics) is to follow Newman's own principle and trace, however briefly, the origins of what is now, still, a highly complex and bureaucratic process. The pope does not suddenly decide to make a saint, and then announce a saint (or a Blessed). It does not work like that at all.

Let me introduce the whole complicated subject by quoting parts of the Interview of the Witness on 18 July 1984 by Father Vincent F. Blehl S.J. of the Historical Commission. The Witness was Monsignor H.F. Davis, and he was then 81 years old.

Q: As is well known, your article 'Newman's Cause' in *Blackfriars*[1] in 1952 led to the introduction of Newman's Cause in 1958. Was there any interest in the Cause prior to that time and, if so, why was the Cause not introduced before 1958?

Witness: Yes there was interest but because of the suspicion of Newman's orthodoxy at the time of the Modernist controversy this issue had to be resolved. Newman had his defenders of course but they were half-hearted. I was able to show, especially with regard to the *Essay on the Development of Christian Doctrine* which was especially used by the Modernists, that Newman was completely orthodox.

Q: This had nothing to do with his sanctity, did it?

Witness: That was not questioned, but only that you cannot canonise someone who is not orthodox.

Q: Your article of 1952 was sent to all the English-speaking Bishops by Fr Philip Lynch, then Superior of the Birmingham Oratory, and the response was favourable. But there is a gap of

---

1   *Blackfriars* is the house magazine of the Dominicans in Oxford. What the Cause is will become clear as readers read on. The "Modernist controversy" occurred before the First World War.

about four years from 1954 to 1958. Was there any reason for this? Was Archbishop Grimshaw cautious or hesitant?

Witness: I do not think Archbishop Grimshaw knew much about Newman but by this time Newman was being highly thought of and Archbishop Grimshaw felt that he was a holy man and should be supported.

Q: Did you encounter anyone, especially anyone in authority, who was opposed to the Cause?

Witness: Cardinal Heenan and Archbishop Dwyer had the same views—their line was: 'What can you produce to show Newman is a saint?' They were willing to listen to the arguments but it seems that the articles published did not move them to the point where they thought he could be declared a saint.

Q: Did you ever encounter anyone who could produce evidence that Newman was not a saint?

Witness: There was a layman, Vincent McClelland, who would take every opportunity to oppose Newman. He seemed to like to stress any point that could be used against Newman.[2]

Q: How was the Historical Commission set up?

Witness: I do not recall.

Q: Did they ever submit anything to you?

Witness: Not that I recall.[3]

Q: What was the reason why the Historical Commission did not submit material?

Witness: No-one was giving himself full-time to the work as you are. We all had our full-time jobs and we had to do the work in our spare time.

Q: Meriol Trevor was getting out her two large volumes at that time and, as I recall, Jonathan Robinson was studying for the priesthood and then became secretary to Cardinal Leger. Father Stephen was editing the *Letters and Diaries of Newman*... So they were all very busy people?

Witness: Yes, that was the chief reason. For any Cause you

---

2 Vincent McClelland's researches sound as if they might be useful to Mr John Cornwell (if he does not already know of them) for his own dark materials.
3 This refers to the first Historical Commission of the late 1950s. Monsignor Davis, the Witness, was then Vice-Postulator of the Cause (and not having much success, it seems).

need a full-time commitment to it and in Newman's Cause particularly so because he lived eighty-nine years and was still active in his later years.

Q: And also because of the enormous mass of material to be gone through in Newman's case?
Witness: Yes.

Q: Have you anything to say about the attitude of those in authority now about Newman?
Witness: My impression since I went to the Council[4] was that everyone was in favour of Newman. The sermon of Pope Paul VI at the beatification of Blessed Dominic[5] was almost like a canonisation of Newman. Almost every Pope in this century spoke of his holiness.

Q: I have heard it said that in Ireland, especially among poor people, there is a tradition that Newman is a Saint?
Witness: Oh yes. They recall that Dr Russell of Maynooth was the only Catholic priest with whom Newman was friendly before he became a Catholic and he was an Irishman.

Q: What about other countries? Is it the same?
Witness: I have travelled in Germany and France and I have been impressed with the love of Newman I have found everywhere. It will be unique if Newman is *not* canonised.

Q: I have found another tradition here in England when I first came in 1957: Some educated people would say 'Newman is a very holy man but not a saint.'
What does this mean? I came to the conclusion that they had a different notion of a saint.
Witness: I think the answer to that is that one ought to have a more universal notion of a saint. There are different saints in different ages: saints of the early Christians, saints of the Middle Ages, saints of modern times. In a way I think Newman does not belong so much to the modern age. He is a Father of the Church. He is St Athanasius rising up again.

Q: In the early days of the Cause I got the impression that

---

4 The Second Vatican Council (1962-1965).
5 Father Dominic Barberi. It does seem a little odd that he should have been beatified so long ago, and Newman not.

what the Congregation of Causes was demanding would take a hundred Newman scholars working a hundred years to fulfil. Was that true?

Witness: Oh yes. I got the impression that it was a Herculean task, certainly, and especially for people doing it in their spare time.

Q: I think that more than anything else explains the slow progress of the Cause?

Witness: Yes.

Here are a few hopefully helpful observations on this series of questions and answers. First of all it is at once obvious that the whole matter of canonisation, beatification and all the rest of it is not simple. There are Commissions, there are Congregations, there are officials, there are enquiries, there are delays; there are prelates who are ignorant (like Archbishop Grimshaw) and prelates who are vaguely hostile (like Cardinal Heenan). There is, to say the least, a great deal of bureaucracy and a great deal of canvassing involved. It all demands a tremendous effort. And as Monsignor Davis says, most people simply do not have the time to put that tremendous effort in. So Causes fall by the wayside. As Newman's Cause fell by the wayside from the time it was first introduced in 1958 until this second wave of activity that culminated in two vast volumes being produced by the Archdiocese of Birmingham in 1989—of which the following heading and (partial) list of contents will give a flavour:

CAUSE OF CANONISATION OF THE SERVANT OF GOD JOHN HENRY CARDINAL NEWMAN (1801-1890)

Report of the Relator of the Cause
Information on the Virtues of the Servant of God
From the Acts of the Diocesan Investigation
    Testimony of 9 Witnesses[6]
    Testimony of 6 ex-officio Witnesses

---

6 Monsignor Davis was Witness No 2. The interrogatory quoted is only an Appendix to the main interview given on oath before the Birmingham Metropolitan Tribunal in 1984.

Testimony of the 3 Historical Commissioners
Rescript of the Sacred Congregation - Arrangements of the Writings
of the Servant of God for the Theological Censors
Vote of the Theological Censors
Decree of the Absence of Unlawful Cult
Etc etc

There are 483 pages in all, and that is only one of the two volumes, which—consider the date of the examination of the witness—must have taken well over five years for the somewhat baffled Jesuit, Father Blehl, to compile.

And then what? Despite Monsignor Davis' rather plaintive cry that "It will be unique if Newman is *not* canonised", another twenty years' delay. So whatever may be thought of the beatification of Newman, it would be rather unfair to suggest that it was hasty, ill-prepared, ill-considered, a bolt out of the papal blue.

Saints and Their Making

It was all so much easier in the old days—the old, old days. Look back at the end of the poetic list in Intermezzo Four. There were the (12) Apostles and the (4) Evangelists; then there were the Martyrs and the Confessors (failed Martyrs, so to speak, who had "confessed" the Christian faith and were ready to face the lions but had been let off). No argument about them—they were obviously Holy Men or Women (which is what *Sanctus* means) and almost equally obviously they had, by their heroic deaths (or wish for heroic deaths), ascended into Heaven.

Then came the Christian convert, the Emperor Constantine, and the end of persecution. No more—at least for the time being—martyrs. The next wave of Holy Men and Women were ascetics: Newman's "holy Monks and Hermits" and "holy Virgins"—friends of God, intercessors with God, links between the community of the living and the community of the dead. In the centuries that followed, as Christianity spread, saints were recognised, often by the local bishops, sometimes by the local kings, often too by popular acclaim, all over Europe. Their burial places became centres of pilgrimage and worship. Churches were built over their tombs, most famously St Peter's above the tomb of St Peter in Rome. Indeed, the Council of Nicaea decreed in 767 AD that all churches must contain an altar stone "having the relics of a saint". The bodies and bones and relics of saints (particularly of martyrs) are "dearer to us than precious stones and finer than gold." Bodies were thus exhumed, often divided and "translated" to an altar, for it was held that their sanctity was present also in their relics.

There was, however, a strict division, at least theologically and officially, between the Worship of God—*latria*—and the veneration due to saints—*dulia* (and above all to the Mother of God, *hyperdulia*). But there was really no control over who became a saint, and how, until a century after the Norman Conquest when Pope Alexander III upbraided King Kol of Sweden for declaring a monk a martyr. The monk had been killed in a drunken brawl at a tavern; and that, Alexander decided, was in no way a witness—martyrdom—to the Faith.

From this landmark imbroglio stemmed the whole process, that still continues, of referring all Causes (applications for sainthood) to Rome—and, one cannot help thinking, quite rightly too. There was a justified crackdown. From 1200 to 1334 only 26 new saints were made or canonised.

There continued to be, and still is, a contrast between what the popes wanted (in Innocent IV's phrase, lives of "continuous uninterrupted virtue", saints as examples of that "hygh holynes of lyvyng") and what the people wanted: miracle workers, thaumaturges, who would help them out. But the centralising rules continued to be tightened, particularly after the Reformation, the Counter-Reformation and the Council of Trent when (in 1588) Pope Sixtus V created the Congregation of Rites, one of fourteen Congregations or departments of state. By Newman's day the whole process of saint-making had become immensely complex, with no fewer than 17 stages of investigations, tribunals, commissions, reports—both locally and in Rome—before the Congregation of Rites, after three different meetings, could issue (if it had so decided, by vote, to do) a solemn decree that evidence existed of the heroic virtues of X, the Servant of God.

Not that "heroic virtues" were enough; they still aren't. But once heroic virtues[7] had been so laboriously established, the Servant of God would be declared Venerable, and the next stage proceeded to (or not, as the case might be). Two miracles were required for beatification, and then two further miracles for canonisation; and the same process, in all its convoluted difficulty, had to be repeated, in all 17 stages (with the addition, of course, of medical tribunals) right from the beginning.

Little wonder, then, that despite certain reforms in 1917, so few saints were made. From 1903 to 1978, seven popes reigned, and there were 98 canonisations in all and only 78 beatifications.

Then came John Paul II, the exotic pope from Poland, and it was all change—or almost. John Paul II canonised 482 men and women and beatified no fewer than 1,337. His view, basically, was that we are all called to be holy, we are all called to be saints of God. And in particular he thought that there should be many more saints in Asia, in Africa, in Oceania—and of many different backgrounds. He canonised a gypsy, El Pele, he canonised, for the first time ever, a married couple. By the reforms of 1983 he reduced the number of miracles required by half (one for beatification, one more for canonisation), the length of time that must elapse between death and the opening of a Cause from fifty years to a mere five, and changed the whole system from the traditional adversarial process dominated by Canon Lawyers to a kind of discursive biographical enquiry dominated by historians. The Postulator became the person who carried the whole Cause onward and paid the bills.[8] The Diocese concentrates on preparing the initial, and vital, *positio*, or sets of documents. The College of Relatorss

---

7   The "heroic virtues" that need to be proved before anyone can be considered for beatification or canonisation are the three theological virtues of faith, hope and charity (all pretty unarguable in Newman's case) and the four cardinal virtues of prudence, justice, fortitude and temperance (almost equally so).

8   Not cheap. The average successful Cause is calculated to cost anywhere between £100,000 and £150,000, which has to be found by those promoting the Cause.

deals with the historical side in Rome, presenting its conclusions to what is now (since the Apostolic Constitution of 1969) no longer the Congregation of Rites but its off-shoot, the Congregation of the Causes of Saints. And, alas, the office of the Promoter of the Faith, the Devil's Advocate so beloved of popular legend, has virtually been sunk into almost total insignificance.

The advantage of these vast changes is clear. The disadvantage, of course, is that there are now so many saints and Blesseds that no Catholic, however devout, can possibly remember them all, still less venerate them all. Once again, as in the early Middle Ages, saints are becoming localised, and inevitably so.

Except perhaps for John Henry Newman, one of the very few who may rightly and deservedly be venerated, if canonised, throughout the Universal Church. As Monsignor Davis put it, "I have travelled in Germany and France and I have been impressed with the love of Newman I have found everywhere." Newman, despite his Anglican background, despite being so English in his Englishness, is not—will not be—an insular saint.

That is if he ever becomes a saint at all, which is probable but by no means certain.

Beatification and Canonisation

What is the difference between them? First of all, of course, *the title*: a Servant of God who is beatified is *Beatus*, happy, Blessed, and a Servant of God who is canonised is *Sanctus*, holy, a saint.

Secondly, and more important, is *the cult*. Basically beatification is *permissive*. It allows the person beatified to be venerated but only locally: in a diocese, or a religious order, or a region, or a nation, or (I suppose) a tribe; it is in a sense therefore restricted, a local cult. Whereas canonisation, the second and final stage, is *prescriptive*, and the person canonised is declared to be a saint to be venerated by the Universal Church. Thus a local bishop will, under the new rules, normally preside, with papal approval, over a beatification; but only the pope in person can preside over a canonisation. (Both the actual rites take place at a Mass, early on, between the *Confiteor* and the *Gloria*; the beatification normally in the diocese concerned; the canonisation invariably at Rome.)

Thirdly, and more interesting, is *the theology*. More interesting because theologians are themselves still arguing. Does canonisation (and beatification) simply mean that the Church recognises X as having lived a holy life on earth? Or does it necessarily mean that X is actually in Heaven? (Or, possibly, still in Purgatory but awaiting Heaven?) Put another way, when the pope pronounces X to be a saint, is this an infallible pronouncement? Is he protected from error?

It is a tricky question. Of course, the normal Catholic assumes, as he or she has always done, that saints are automatically in Heaven. But what if a pope canonises, in good faith, a person who is afterwards proved to have been very far from virtuous? Graham Greene loved to provoke by saying that to be a great saint one had to be a great sinner, which always seemed to me in his case just a self-indulgent aphorism. Certainly St Paul, St Augustine and indeed St Francis were all notable sinners though their later sanctity seems beyond question. But what, for example, of St Maria Goretti, canonised by Pope Pius XII in 1950, 48 years after her death in 1902? She was, aged twelve, raped and murdered by a neighbouring peasant boy aged only eighteen. She became the most popular symbol of heroic virginity in post-war Italy, dying almost a martyr, not exactly for her faith but in defence of Christian virtue.

Then in 1985 a left-wing Italian journalist Giordano Bruno Guerri published a book entitled *Poor Assassin, Poor Saint: The True Story of Maria Goretti*. His argument, based on both Church documents and the state trial of the eighteen-year-old, was that the whole saint-making process was in this case flawed. He even suggested that Maria had willingly consented to intercourse (but not, presumably, to being murdered). There was a tremendous fuss with, at one stage, Guerri threatening to sue the Vatican for defamation. It all died down. But it does point to the possibility—to put it no stronger than that—that a person declared officially a saint may later be discovered not really to have been one at all.

Of course, the counter-argument put forward by those theologians who hold that the pope, in canonising a saint to be venerated by the Universal Church is speaking *ex cathedra*, is that such a declaration will therefore be protected by the Holy Spirit from error. Yet even the First Vatican Council was careful not to specify canonisation as necessarily involving an infallible pronouncement.

What is certain, though, what all theologians (as far as I can tell) agree on is that beatification is definitely not an infallible declaration. Therefore the proclamation of Newman as Blessed could logically one day—unlikely though it seems in practice—be recognised as wrong.

Perhaps in all this enthralling intellectual confusion the best thing is to cling onto the wise old monsignor's point; when he states: "There are different saints in different ages: saints of the early Christians, saints of the Middle Ages, saints of modern times." All sorts of saints, in fact, and it is difficult therefore to pin down any precise definition, to set any perfect limits.

Save, of course, that the Church still insists on one miracle for the first stage, beatification; and a second miracle for the second stage, canonisation. Thus, to return to my original point, with only one miracle claimed Newman's Cause may—as many others have done (the Blessed Dominic Barberi's, for instance, and more recently Mother Teresa's)—stick at beatification alone. In which case Newman will **not** become a saint.

Newman's Miracle

Way back in 1938 a Flemish-speaking Belgian, Mother (as she became) Julia Verhaeghe, founded a rather unusual religious organisation with a rather unusual name: "The Spiritual Family The Work", combining priests, nuns and laity. Possibly Mother Julia was originally inspired by Newman. Certainly The Work now runs International Newman Centres in Rome, in Jerusalem, in Bregenz in Austria, in Budapest and at Littlemore.

In April 1990 the International Newman Centre in Via Aurelia organised a three-day Newman symposium in Rome, on the hundredth anniversary of Newman's death. It was quite an event. The present pope, then Cardinal Ratzinger, a great fan of Newman, attended and presented the delegates to the then pope. "I welcome all of you," said John Paul II, "and thank you for drawing attention through your celebration to the great English Cardinal's special place in the history of the Church."

Early the following year, the pope followed up his remarks. He accepted the hard-working Father Blehl's *positio*, his elaborate account—passed on to the Holy Father by the Cardinal Prefect of the Congregation for the Causes of Saints after the requisite examinations and votes—of Newman's heroic virtues, and in January 1991 declared John Henry Newman, the Servant of God, to be Venerable. The preliminary exam had, so to speak, been passed. All it needed now was a miracle.

That same January Jack Sullivan, an American of Irish descent whose family had come over to Boston, USA, with the Kennedys, became chief magistrate of Plymouth District Court in Massachusetts, where the Pilgrim Fathers had landed. Born in 1938 and married to a practising Catholic (which his own parents had ceased to be) in 1969, he and his wife Carol had adopted two children and then (almost miraculously, perhaps) had a third naturally, in 1981. There was nothing particularly out of the ordinary about Jack Sullivan, a decent American citizen, except perhaps that he was dyslexic (and therefore clearly no intellectual). Also, at the age of twenty, he had briefly attempted to be a priest, but after two years at a seminary had decided he had no vocation, and switched to law. But in 1998, at the age of sixty, he reverted. That is to say, he decided to become a married deacon, and started a four-year part-time training course.

Then, on Tuesday 6 June 2000, he woke up with tremendous pain in his back and legs. A CAT scan revealed that his spine was herniated causing severe stenosis in both legs. An operation seemed essential. He could walk, just, but hunched, with his head bent towards the ground.

On 26 June, at home, flicking through TV channels, on Eternal Word Television Network he came across a programme about the life and teachings of Newman. "I had heard about Cardinal Newman but I did not know much about his life," he later said. It seems weird, but somehow weirdly suitable, that the Newman miracle should result from a chance encounter via a technological "miracle" of which Newman in his lifetime would never have had the faintest conception.

On the screen, being interviewed by an American priest, was the most noted Newman scholar of our times (at present parish priest of Burford in Oxfordshire where he preaches witty as well as inspiring sermons on Sundays), Father Ian Ker. He mentioned *en passant* the need for a miracle if Newman was ever to be beatified, and at the end of the programme the TV audience was asked to send accounts of any extraordinary experiences or healings resulting from a prayer of intercession to Newman to the then Postulator of the Cause, Father Paul Chavasse, provost of The Oratory, Birmingham, England.

So far so good. A chance encounter via television, and "I felt a very strong compulsion to pray to Cardinal Newman with all my heart. I didn't pray particularly for healing but for greater persistence and courage in my life. Immediately after my prayer I suddenly experienced a new and uplifting sense of trust and confidence."

Next morning the pain had gone, and Sullivan found he could walk almost normally. But on 18 July a myelogram ordered by a neurologist at a Boston hospital showed the spinal chord dangerously affected, with a very high risk of complete lower body paralysis unless surgery was performed. Neither the neurologist nor a specialist in spinal surgery whom Sullivan was referred to, Dr Banco of New England Baptist Hospital, could explain the lack of pain or the patient's continued ability to walk upright.

One of the medical requirements that the Catholic Church insists on is that cures, if they are to be considered miraculous, should be not merely inexplicable by current medical science but permanent (insofar as mortal man's cures ever can be permanent) rather than merely temporary, a blip. And, to cut a long story short, on Sunday 22 April 2001—that is to say ten months after the first inexplicable "cure"—the pain returned worse and more debilitating than ever, despite all the patient's continual prayers to Newman. The previous "cure", then, had been, though apparently inexplicable, temporary and therefore was never, indeed could never be, claimed as miraculous.

Sullivan continued his third-year deacon's training as a medical intern, but in a wheelchair. "I prayed continuously to Cardinal Newman that the Lord might give me strength and courage to continue, dedicating my hospital ministry to him." By June 2001 the latest X-rays showed his condition was far too serious for his court work or the (twice-weekly) medical internship to be allowed to continue. On 9 August he was finally operated on by Dr Banco. His lower spine was found to be badly ruptured, and the *dura mater*, the membrane surrounding the spinal cord, badly torn and leaking fluids. The surgery was therefore difficult but successful. The post-operative pain was so great that, two days later, the patient had to have morphine administered every few hours. To move to the edge of the bed was agony. The prognosis was for a long and painful post-operative recovery that would take at least several months, probably close to a year.

Then on 15 August, six days after the operation, Jack Sullivan, so to speak, like the character in the gospel, took up his bed and walked. In his own words, "Suddenly I felt a very warm sensation over my body, a sense of real peace and joy. Then I felt a surge of strength, and I was completely free of the crippling pain… My healing became remarkably and unexplainably accelerated in one moment of time." He got up and walked. "I just wanted to walk and walk." The hospital agreed to discharge him, Carol came to pick him up, he got dressed, tried to walk out of the hospital unaided, but was told he could only be discharged if he got back into his wheelchair and was pushed out. (Fear of a lawsuit against the hospital if he tumbled over, I suppose). "From that moment to this day in 2008 the pain has never once returned and I continue to walk normally with no restriction and with full mobility."

That was the miracle: the sudden release from long-lasting pain, the inexplicable nature of the sudden release and its permanency. Dr Banco told Sullivan he had never seen anything like it, and had no medical explanation at all for it. The ex-patient decided to write a letter about it all to Father Paul Chavasse at the Birmingham Oratory. Father Chavasse notified by email the provost of the Pittsburgh Oratory, Pennsylvania that he, the Postulator for the Cause and his advisers, thought that the story of Sullivan's healing sounded as if it deserved further investigation. This was in September 2002, and things proceeded from there.

First of all the bishop of the diocese in which the alleged miracle occurred has to set up a tribunal with two sub-committees, one scientific—to examine in detail the cure, the patient, the treatment, how the healing has occurred, its permanency—and the other, theological, to establish whether it came about by intercession of the candidate for beatification: in this case Newman. Then if both sub-committees (after examination of witnesses and all the rest of it) are satisfied, the *positio,* the tribunal's report, goes to Rome, to the Congregation for the Cause of Saints where first the *Consulta Medica*, a body of five medical experts, considers the evidence, and then seven theologians. Yet more votes, checks, officials, bishops and cardinals are involved before the results, if favourable, are passed up to the pope. (If unfavourable, of course, at any stage, the process stops there until another miracle is alleged, reported, investigated and, possibly, finally approved.) Then the pope alone takes the final decision.

In Sullivan's case Cardinal Sean O'Malley set up the diocesan tribunal in Boston. It was not until November 2006, four years later, that all the documents were forwarded to Rome. The Roman processes took another two and a half years. Then, finally, on 3 July 2009, the Decree of Beatification of John Henry Newman was issued by Pope Benedict XVI. Jack Sullivan must have been thrilled.

An American writer, Kenneth Woodward, obviously fascinated by the whole business, published in 1991 a book entitled *Making Saints*. He was particularly curious about why it had taken so long for Newman to be beatified/canonised. He came to England, and Rome, to investigate. He put the delays down largely to the inexperience of the Catholic Church in England in setting about making saints, to the worries of the bishops (and indeed of the Oratory Fathers,) about the expense and the bother and to Monsignor Davis who set it all going being "too gentle". Progress he attributed mainly to the American Jesuits in the person of the (rather severe) Father Blehl. They had, he implied, the money, the drive and the enthusiasm that the plodding English lacked. As long ago as 1973, he reveals, Pope Paul VI was asking the Oratorians how they were getting along, and hoping to beatify Newman in the Holy Year of 1975.   A failure.

As for John Paul II he wanted to be the pope to beatify, and perhaps even canonise, Newman. Again it was a failure because, as Mr Woodward puts it, "Until someone comes forward with a demonstrable miracle through Newman's intercession, his cause will remain in a state of arrested development." Even popes cannot produce miracles at, as Mr Woodward might have phrased it, their say-so.

It seems somehow most fitting that, in the end, it should be Pope Benedict who beatifies Newman, and therefore that the requisite miracle and its confirmation[9] should not have occurred till his papacy. Why? Because Pope Benedict, much more so than the austere Paul VI or the ebullient John Paul II, is not only an admirer of Newman but the same sort of man—an academic, a university professor, a

---

9   The miracle in itself may not appear immensely miraculous—after all it was a cure only after an operation—but there are three things to be said against those who may attempt to deny it. First of all, on Newman's own (favourite) argument of antecedent probability it seems unlikely that after all this time and all these investigations the Church authorities should fix on a miracle that is in any way doubtful in itself.

Secondly, will fair-minded readers refer back to Newman's own criteria (in Intermezzo II, with reference to St Philip Neri's miracles) and apply the criteria Newman lays down to his, and Jack Sullivan's, own case?

Thirdly, this is of course not the only miraculous claim put forward. It seems that there have been hundreds of "graces" or "favours" reported. But obviously it was felt to be the best. I myself in the course of writing this book have heard of one case (in England, not America this time) that involves an inexplicable cure of a non-Catholic (but have been forbidden by my informant to go into any detail). I think Mr Sullivan may have convinced because it seems (present report again from a friend who has met him) he is obviously a very reliable and decent man; clearly one would not want to put forward anyone in any way hysterical, over-emotional or prone to exaggeration. He is also alive, well and apparently going to come over to England and serve as a deacon at the beatification ceremony—and no doubt face what Prince Philip would call the vultures at the same time.

courteous yet determined character[10], above all an intellectual. Indeed, one elderly English priest has, it appears, privately described Benedict as a "new Athanasius raised up by the Lord"—which sounds a touch Cromwellian, but would certainly have won Newman's approval.

One feels the two men would, if they had been contemporaries, whether now or then, have got on remarkably well together. The pope obviously has a great deal in common with the admired Dr Döllinger—the Bavarian background and tradition—and both he and Newman have/had a great love of music. Benedict's early studies were focused on that other Doctor of the Church, St Augustine of Hippo rather than St Athanasius, but two at least of his tutors were known for their studies of Newman, and he himself has certainly absorbed *The Essay on Development of Christian Doctrine* and has often referred to its significance. But perhaps most fitting of all in present circumstances is his view of the saints as intercessors. When Benedict was installed as pope at St Peter's on 24 April 2005, he preached a sermon following the chanting, in procession, of the Litany of the Saints:

"And now at this moment I must assume this enormous task. How can I do this? How will I be able to do this? I, too, can say with renewed conviction I am not alone. All the saints of God are there to protect me, to sustain me and to carry me."

And soon, amidst all these saints of God, may be John Henry Newman. It seems fitting indeed that—if this does occur—he should sustain and protect a pope whom he, in so many ways, so much resembles.

---

10 As indeed is the present Archbishop of Canterbury, Dr Rowan Williams. What would be truly a miracle, and an earth shattering second miracle, would be if, via Newman's intercession, the Archbishop of Canterbury were during the Pope's visit to announce that the Anglican schism was at long last at an end and that he was personally leading his flock back into union with Rome. Unlikely perhaps. But, as Newman said, miracles do happen in every age of the Church.

Mr Woodward ends his chapter on Newman with:

> Who can say that an acceptable miracle will ever be found? The question is, of course, does it matter? What can canonisation add to a man whose influence is equal to that of any other saint created by the church in the last four hundred years?
>
> What matters is that much as the church needs saints like Newman, the canonisation process still does not readily comprehend the worth of the intellectually gifted.
>
> Religious intellectuals and artists mediate Christ in ways that only powerful thought and art can do and therefore serve as models of holiness within high culture. Their asceticism is not the asceticism of the cloistered monk, their insights are not the insights of the mystic, their suffering, though often great, is not the suffering of the martyr.

Very true, very well put. But now it looks as if thanks to the perhaps unlikely combination of Mr Jack Sullivan of Boston, Mass., and Pope Benedict XVI of the Vatican, Rome, that unfortunate gap in the Catholic panoply is about to be triumphantly bridged.

There is just one final question that remains. Turn back for a moment, please, to Monsignor Davis' testimony—towards the end where he says:

"In a way I think Newman does not belong to the modern age. [Well, maybe what was the modern age in 1984 is no longer the same modern age a quarter of a century later: each reader will have his or her own opinion on this.] He is a Father of the Church. He is St Athanasius rising up again."

I think Monsignor Davis meant to say, or at least meant to imply, a Doctor of the Church. There were eight of them originally, the great surviving link between the Orthodox and the Catholic Churches, three Greek—Basil the Great, Gregory the Theologian and John Chrysostom (John "of the golden tongue")—and five Latin: St Ambrose, St Augustine, St Jerome, St Gregory the Great and, of course, Newman's own favourite, St Athanasius. There are thirty-three now (they have gradually been added to over the ages) including St Thomas Aquinas, St John of the Cross and the only Englishman so far, the Venerable Bede.

Doctors of the Universal Church they are officially called, and they form, as it were, an aristocracy of the intellect among the saints of the Church, noted both for the greatness of their learning and the holiness of their lives. To be proclaimed a Doctor of the Church is the highest accolade, the deepest bow to intellectual greatness that can be bestowed by the Church on earth upon a select band of the Church in heaven.

It would be a great and glorious thing indeed if John Henry Newman were to be recognised as the thirty-fourth member of this celestial Academy. Perhaps it will be not too long delayed; and, whatever he may or may not have thought of one day becoming a saint, there can be almost no doubt that this is one enormous honour that Newman would have been only too proud and delighted to accept.

Oremus.

Epilogue

THE PILGRIMS TO ROME.
(AFTER CHAUCER.)

Whanne that ye firste of April breedeth jokès
On boys and girls and simple full-grown folkès,
To seken out what they mote never findè,
Legs from the lame, and eyesight from the blindè -
Whan, that conceit our clerkes eke and our cittès
Enspirèd hath, out of their shallow wittès;
And chaunting curates maken melodie
Whereof nought understanden you or I -
So Oxford tractes prike them in their corages, -
Then longen folkes to go on Pilgramages,
And unwashed priests from many a foreign lande
Men may beholden walkinge in the Strande;
And clerkes, and squiers, and youngè ladyes eke,
They wenden forth the Churche of Rome to seke.

Methought that in that seson, on a date,
In Fleet Streete at mine office as I lay
Of Pilgrimes I beheld a compagnie
That on their viage unto Rome wente bye;
And I wold tellen, as it seemèd me,
What sort they weren, and of what degree,
And eke in what arraie that they were inne, -
And at a Lord then will I firste beginne.

This rather wonderful pastiche comes from *Punch or The London Charivaria*, at the time of the "Papal Aggression"[1] when feelings ran higher against Popery than ever they had since the fearsome Gordon

---

1 In 1850 (See Chapter IV). This pastiche was published in late 1850, in Vol XIX of *Punch*, where readers can find, if they wish, the full text—there is a set of verses for each of the twelve pilgrims; thus five are not included here.

Riots of seventy years earlier. The "characters" that follow all (or almost all) appear in the preceding chapters. It is noticeable that the first Pilgrim, the Good Earl, is treated gently, almost with respect, and that the cardinal at the end, is let off pretty lightly—perhaps after he had appealed to the "good sense" of his fellow-Englishmen.

Ye Lord - A Lord there was - and that a worthy man
That, fro the time his college life beganne,
Was wont to talken of the good olde timès,
And thereof wrote he and eke publish'd rhymès,
Him seemèd it a sin that pourè elvès
Should thinken or should redden for themselvès
He woldè that the people should be goode,
Nor troublen them neither for faithe nor foode;
For faithe, sith Holy Churche should still their qualmès,
For foode, sith Lordès should give them almès.
At Rome he was when Holy Week begonne
After St Januarius wolde he ronne
To see his bloode melt - and it did him paine
That chemists wolde the miracle explaine.
At the Pope's feet eke wolde he louten low
To kissen of the Holy Father's toe.
His Hall, I wot, was silly *Pugin's* glory.
For therein had he made an Oratorie
With saintes the ugliest that mote be seene;
Poundès it coste two thousand and fifteene
In briefe, his thought was by his life to prove
How that the worlde no businesse hath to move,
So to its motion he did shutte his eyes;
Yet he was worthy, though he was not wise
And of his port as meke as is a maide;
He never yet no villainie y-sayde,
Save of the lettere that Lord John did write.
He was a very perfect, gentle wighte.

The reference in the last line but one is to the prime minister Lord John Russell's notorious letter to the Bishop of Durham. The cost of the gothicised Alton Towers (l.20) sounds about right for the time. In *The Illustration* the top-hatted Lord rides immediately behind the cardinal (as is only befitting for the Premier Earl of England and Ireland).

> **Ye Squire -** With him there rode his friend - a batchelere,
> An Exquisite, and a Young Englandere
> Within St Stephen's had he showed his strengthe;
> His speeches were much talked of - for their lengthe
> Of ballades he was author, two or three,
> In Annuals and eke in Manuscrit,
> In Saintès praise; but his look seemèd meet
> Less for *St James* than for St James his street
> Sweet-scented were the lockès on his head,
> His tie was full of flowers, white and red;
> Lounging he was or flirting all the daie;
> Up to the Derbie rode he every Maie;
> Well could he talk of fasting and penaunce
> To maides, between the figure of the daunce;
> And from the hollow world within the cloistre
> Threaten to shut himself, as in an oystre.
> Whereat the gentle ladyes woldè flush;
> And with a tender sigh wolde bid him hush:
> Courteous he was - at parties serviceable;
> And out of church spent much time in the stable.

Is this meant to be Ambrose Phillipps? It sounds in part more like jabs at Lord George Bentinck. Ambrose was not, I think, a racing man, and was surely never in Parliament. But Lord George was, equally surely, not a religious man, certainly not a Roman.

> **Ye Bishope -** A Bishope was there eke, a cholericke man,
> To put down heresye with booke and ban;
> And heresye full shorte definèd he, -

"Heresye is the differing from me."
Unto the texte he wolde not lend his eares
That sayeth "Blessed are ye peace-makeres,"
Or claimed himself that blessing, with increase,
"Because," quoth he, "I make knaves hold their peace."
Obedience unto Bishops he wolde preche,
But to resist Archbishops still did teache;
And, eke, he was a prosecutor tight, -
For if one of his parsons dared to write,
Or preche against his will - for Churche's glory
He clapped him straightway into Consistorie.
In quibbling and in splitting of a hair,
Was all his luste - and costs he wolde not spare.

Who could this be? Bishop Baines of Prior Park, possibly? Surely not Bishop Ullathorne of Birmingham? Or is it a dig at an Anglican bishop whom Mr Punch fears might "go over"? The face, staring out at us, ought to be recognisable—and no doubt immediately was to *Punch*'s readers.

Ye Clerke of Oxenford - A Clerke there was of Oxenforde, also,
That shoulde have been at Rome long time ago;
Well coulde he logike choppe, and fairly make
The worstè cause the beste, for Churche's sake.
And he had gotten him a benefice,
And, though an Anglican, he was not nice,
To lead his flocke righte cunningly from home
Until he hadde them folded safe in Rome.
He recked more of bowed back and bended knee,
Than of an uprighte life and honestie;
Of altars sette with candles, and such showes,
Than of the light a pure ensample throwes.
And younge mene that did with him scolaie
He thoughte it dutiful to lead astraie;
Sounding in hollow reasons was his speche,
And well could be pervert, and well misteche.

Our hero—here accused, very much like Socrates by the Athenians, of corrupting the young with his sophistries. Identifiable by his flat hat and spectacles in the illustration, but not (for some reason) by his most prominent feature, his extremely beaky nose. Too impressive?

Ye Curate - With him there rode a Curate, fresshe and faire,
In coate full long, and smoothely parted haire;
At the West End, there, in a faire chapelle,
From curates rounde aboute he bore the belle.
With ladies olde and younge he was the rage,
Both for his fastinge and his fayre language.
He was a stoute ecclesiologist,
And had his chancelle sette oute, as him list,
With altar, and sedilia, and cross,
Piscina, roode-lofte, awmrie, and rere-dos,
He sette much store by bowinges Weste and Easte,
And kneelinges of ye people and ye prieste;
For prieste he did him clepe, and held it taunte
To be styled Clergyman and Protestaunte.
Fine were his handes, and fayre white was his skin,
As was the surplice he wold prechen in;
Upon ye slie heard he confession
From youngè women, that wolde flop them downe,
And poure their little sinnes into his eare,
That the poore Curate mote not help but heare.
Though he saide nay, a sainte they made him still,
And canonised their Curate, 'gainst his wille.
So with a humble looke, and a proude hearte,
This sely Curate he did ride aparte,
Y-wrapped in a gowne of selfe-conceite.

This, the most vicious sketch of all, is probably of Father Faber, in the West End at Brompton Oratory—and only too fashionable.

Ye Limnere and ye Architecte - They hadden with them eke
a young Limnere,
An Architecte, besides, that was his frere,
To whom their arte advance did seeme to lack;
For why? Because that it wolde not goe backe.
To be original, they did upholde,
Artistes mote do what artistes did of olde
This one made churches, wherein that did painte
Many a stiff-necked nunne and long-toed sainte,
So rude and harshe, men mote sweeare they did see
Ye thirteenthe, in ye nineteenthe centuries;
And o'er such werkès each did praise ye other,
And Architecte o'er Limnere made much pother,
And Limnere in his turn o'er Architecte:
Humbuggès were they both, I sore suspecte.
To Rome they rode, so they informèd me,
For childe-like Faithe, and early Pietie.

Pugin of course is the Architect. Who the Limnere is, with his
easel and brushes, I cannot be quite sure. Pugin, unhatted, rides in
front of the Limnere.

Ye Cardinale - Their leader was a stout carl, for the nones;
Full bigge he was of brawn, and eke of bones;
A redde hatte had he, and redde were his hose;
A pastoral entuned he through this nose,
That from ye Vatican had lately come;
And therewithal he ledde this route to Rome.

Wiseman, naturally—in full fig.

Bibliography

This short biography of Newman makes no claim to be a work of original research. It stands on the shoulders of other biographies (not only of Newman) and owes a great debt to these books and to their authors, which hereby I most gratefully acknowledge.

The only biography I deliberately did *not* consult of those listed below—neither this nor his other works as perhaps the greatest Newman scholar of our age—is that of Father Ian Ker, for fear that it would have such an influence that in effect all I would be writing would be a condensed version of his masterpiece.

Biographies of Newman

The Life of John Henry Cardinal Newman - Wilfred Ward (2 Vols: London 1912)
The classic life, devoted almost entirely, however, to the years *after* his conversion.

Young Mr Newman - Maisie Ward (Sheed & Ward, 1948)
By William Ward's daughter. Fills in the early years. Readers will notice that I have "borrowed" her book title for a chapter title of my own.

Newman: The Pillar of the Cloud - Meriol Trevor (2 Vols: Macmillan, 1962)
Newman: Light in Winter
Miss Trevor was on the Historical Commission set up by the Birmingham Archdiocesan Tribunal. She followed these books up with a Life of Philip Neri.

Newman and His Age - Sheridan Gilley (Darton, Longman & Todd, 1990)
Extremely accessible modern biography, which I used as my bedside reading while writing this book, and hereby most gratefully acknowledge all the help and information I derived from it.

John Henry Newman: A Biography - Ian Ker (Clarendon Press 1988)
A massive 762 pages, the great modern biography. Father Ker also
co-edited the first four volumes of Newman's *Diaries and Letters* and
the Penguin Classic edition of the *Apologia* (with introduction)—and
has written innumerable articles on Newman. He is, furthermore,
indirectly responsible, via his American television interview, for
Newman's Miracle (See Chapter Seven) and, thus, his Beatification.

There are many other biographies of Newman, in many different
styles and languages; and innumerable books about him. Three
shelves, no less, of the London Library, groan under their weight.
I list here therefore only the ones I have particularly used and add
other biographies and general books.

God's Architect: Pugin and the Building of Romantic Britain - Rosemary
Hill (Allen Lane, 2007)
A vast and fascinating study; with lots, of course, about the Good
Earl, Pugin's patron.

The Catholic Families - Mark Bence Jones (Constable, 1992)
The news of the sad death of the author, great authority on Irish
Georgian architecture, has just come through as this book was going
to press.

The Stripping of the Altars - Eamon Duffy (Yale University Press, 1992)
The famous account of the Reformation in England—and times
before.

Conscience and Papacy - Stanley L Jaki (Michigan, 2002)
Text, and notes, introduction and forceful comments, on the *Letter
to the Duke of Norfolk*.

Making Saints - Kenneth Woodward (Chatto & Windus, 1991)
Much used for my last chapter, as was the Catholic Truth Society
Pamphlet, *Cardinal Newman: The Story of a Miracle* by Peter Jennings.

The Life of William Ewart Gladstone - John Morley (3 Vols: Macmillan, 1903)
The great classic.

The Life of Cardinal Manning - E. S. Purnell (2 Vols: Macmillan, 1895)
Published very soon—perhaps too soon—after Manning's death.

Newman and Gladstone: Centennial Essays (ed. J. D. Bastable, Dublin, 1978)
Not quite what it promises. Only one essay on the title subject.

The Convert Cardinals: Newman and Manning - David Newsome (John Murray, 1993)

Nicholas Wiseman - Brian Fothergill (Faber & Faber, 1962)

Kingsley versus Newman: The Full Text (Oxford University Press, 1913)
Comprises the correspondence in full, the pamphlets and the *Apologia* in its original version. Fascinating.

A Tribute to Newman: Irish Essays (Browne & Nelson, 1945)
Includes a fine essay by Roger McHugh and another on John Hungerford Pollen and the University Church by C. P. Curran.

It does not seem necessary to include the vast list of Newman's own writings in this short bibliography; nor the enormous amount of books about the Oxford Movement (of which Professor Owen Chadwick's, mentioned on p. 47, is the one I personally found the most interesting). There are biographies of Keble, Pusey, and almost all the other Oxford figures mentioned, including Hurrell Froude, Whately and Hope-Scott. Martin Murphy has written a most interesting monograph on Blanco White. The list is almost endless and no doubt will now go on and into the future...

The Thought of Pope Benedict XVI - Adrian Nichols OP (Burns & Oates, 2007)
An extremely erudite book, with a most informative first chapter on "The Bavarian Background".

Acknowledgements

As always to the reverent London Library and its ever-helpful staff for the kick-off point. Then to Johnnie Rous for his hospitality and use of the splendid Victorian library at Clovelly Court; to the Abbot and Community for their continued hospitality and the use of the daunting but comprehensive monastic library at Downside; to the Master of St Benet's Hall in St Giles' at Oxford for the use of the almost cosy little college library there during a peaceful and productive week; and finally, passing the finishing post, to the sisters of The Work who so beautifully run Newman College and its atmospheric contents out at Littlemore and to the fathers of the Birmingham Oratory and in particular to Father Richard Duffield (now the Actor of the Cause) for a fascinating tour of Rednal and Birmingham—a city I am abashed to say I had never previously set foot in.

Above all, of course, profound acknowledgements for their help, via these libraries, to the authors, both dead and alive—and including in the first place John Henry Newman himself—who have written so many books and articles and essays about the great man and his times. Among which this effort will now, hopefully, find its little niche.

Index